Michael Henderson was born in Lancashire, edu~~~
Derbyshire, and lives in London. A well-known writer on sport,
and the arts, he has worked for the *Times*, the *Guardian*, and
the *Daily Mail*, and was cricket correspondent of the *Daily
Telegraph*. He also writes about music for the *Spectator*. His
interests include German music, Dutch paintings, Russian
novels, American films, French wine and English ale.

50 PEOPLE WHO FOULED UP FOOTBALL

MICHAEL HENDERSON

Illustrations by
NICOLA JENNINGS

Constable . London

Constable and Robinson
3 The Lanchesters
162 Fulham Palace Road
London W6 9ER
www.constablerobinson.com

First published in the UK in hardback by Constable,
an imprint of Constable & Robinson Ltd 2009
This paperback edition published in 2010.

A copy of the British Library cataloguing in Publication Data is
available from the British Library.

ISBN 978-1-84901-269-0

Printed and bound in the EU

3 5 7 9 10 8 6 4

In memory of my father, Rev. James Henderson,
who loved football

Contents

viii CONTENTS

Acknowledgements

The thoughts in this book are mine but they arose from years of lively conversations with friends, usually in places where strong drink is taken. I must therefore thank Philippe Auclair, Patrick Barclay, Conor Brennan, Howard Davies, Mike Dickson, Mike Ellison, Neil Hallam, Daniel Harding, Robert Madge, Gerald Mortimer, Michael Parkinson, Giles Phillips, Nick Rowe, Colin Shindler, Clive Toye, Chris Travers and Bob Willis. For one specific suggestion I am indebted to Adrian Deevoy. Thanks also to Andreas Campomar, and to those 'Blest Pair of Sirens', Ludwig and Franz, who are always there.

Preface:
England and the World Cup

The English, or, to be absolutely scrupulous, the British, have given the world most of the sports that are worth playing. The world gave thanks, caught up with their tutors, and moved briskly on. In cricket England have not been the strongest team in the world since the 1950s. The rugby players did win a World Cup in 2003, it is true, and British golfers have conquered the world, but tennis is a dead loss, and, at the highest level, our footballers have been found wanting time and time again.

We are not supposed to show our sportsmen in that unflattering a light. The Premier League is a global hit, with the world's leading players beating a path to our island. Yet facts keep getting in the way. England has won the World Cup once, in 1966, when the tournament was staged here. Apart from that success, achieved in a pragmatic manner that did not meet with universal approval, the national team has reached the last four of the competition on only one other occasion. A useful comparison is with Germany, a European country of equivalent pedigree, whose players have won three World Cups and appeared in the final on seven occasions.

On account of differences with FIFA, the international game's governing body, England did not appear in the final stages of a World Cup until 1950. Having been admitted to the tournament, held that year in Brazil, they took their leave in the most abject manner, losing 1–0 to the United States in a qualifying match. 'Did you play that day?' somebody asked Sir Alf Ramsey years later. 'I was the only one who did,' he replied.

The decade after the Second World War was a great age for English football. Never before or since has our game enjoyed such an abundance of outstanding players. Stanley Matthews, Tom Finney, Nat Lofthouse, Tommy Lawton, Wilf Mannion, Len Shackleton, Stan Mortensen and Billy Wright are embedded in football's folklore. Crowds saw the first glimpses of John Haynes and Bobby Charlton, while the Munich air disaster of February 1958 ended the lives of Roger Byrne, Tommy Taylor and Duncan Edwards as Manchester United were getting the measure of Europe.

Who knows how different the World Cups in 1958 and 1962 would have been with the United players leading the way? We shall never know, alas. What is beyond dispute is that, even with such marvellous players available, England failed to leave much of a mark in 1954, when Fritz Walter's West Germany eventually overcame the great Hungarians, and four years later, when Brazil, with the seventeen-year-old Pelé newly installed – a king-in-waiting – won the first of their five trophies.

After the 1962 World Cup in Chile, Walter Winterbottom stepped down, to be replaced as England manager by Ramsey, who had just won the League Championship with Ipswich Town.

He had three years to prepare for the World Cup, which was being held in England. Home advantage certainly played a part in their success, for they were not the most gifted team in the tournament, any more than West Germany had been in 1954, or Italy were in 2006.

Ramsey had three trump cards up his sleeve: one was Gordon Banks, the finest goalkeeper in the world; indeed, as fine a goalie as any team has known. 'Banks of England' was a true great. His two other great players were the Bobbys – Moore and Charlton. In the single most important act of his decade-long career as manager, Ramsey appointed Moore, then just twenty-two, as his captain, and saw him mature into a superb leader. In Charlton's case he helped turn the left-winger into a midfield general, who ended his England career with forty-nine goals – a record that still stands today.

That July day, when England played in strawberry-jam shirts, was the greatest occasion in the history of the country that invented the game. Since then the tale has been one of chronic underachievement. Or has it? England took a splendid team to Mexico in 1970, where they lost 1–0 to Brazil in a qualifying match that has achieved classic status, before squandering a two-goal lead against the Germans after Ramsey withdrew Charlton in the heat of Leon. Yet, however good England were, the Germans were hardly less talented. And, as for Brazil, surely it cannot be gainsaid that the side led by Carlos Alberto, featuring the skills of Tostão, Gerson, Jairzinho and Rivelino, as well as Pelé, was the finest ever to play the game.

And did England fail to live up to expectations when they were edged out of qualification for the 1974 tournament by Poland? To some extent they did. Ramsey had some excellent players at his disposal, yet the game was changing in Europe, and he seemed unaware of, if not exactly indifferent to, the modifications wrought by the Dutch and Germans. Poland, remember, finished third in 1974, even without Wlodek Lubanski, the inside forward – to use a pleasingly old-fashioned term – who had orchestrated their victory against England in Katowice the year before.

After Ramsey had been sacked, and replaced by Don Revie, England fared little better. Injury deprived Revie of two important midfield players, Colin Bell and Gerry Francis, but he did not play his hand cleverly, and defeat in Rome in 1976 cost England another qualification. Italy did well in Argentina, beating the hosts, who went on to win the tournament, so once again England's conquerors had established the right to play on the biggest stage. By then England had found another coach. Revie, who was not cut out for international management, skedaddled to the United Arab Emirates, who waved a fat cheque under his nose in the summer of 1977.

A decade in the wilderness ended in 1982 when Ron Greenwood's team went to Spain, and turned up few trees. Kevin Keegan, their star player in the late 1970s, was in decline, and Gary Lineker had yet to emerge. When Lineker did flower, in Mexico four years later, England found Diego Maradona, who was granted exceptional licence by an indulgent referee, too hard to handle. Lineker was still a key figure in 1990, when

England reached the last four for only the second time. There wasn't much to separate Bobby Robson's team from Franz Beckenbauer's Germans, only the penalties missed by Chris Waddle and Stuart Pearce, who had both played superbly. England has not always deserved sympathy. On that occasion they were valiant in defeat.

The World Cup of 1994 took place in the United States without England, who failed to get past the Netherlands in the qualifying group. In France four summers later Argentina won an eventful game on penalties after David Beckham had been sent off for a petulant flick. That was the game in which Michael Owen declared his talent with a fine individual goal, which marked him down as one for the big occasion. He proved it again against Brazil in the quarter final of 2002, giving England a lead they failed to hold against 10 opponents after Ronaldinho was dismissed. It was not underachievement: England was simply not good enough.

An odd notion had taken hold by now, of a 'golden generation' of players who would carry England to glory. Expectations were absurdly high in 2006, when the England party, swollen by a ludicrous assortment of female companions, took over the fashionable town of Baden Baden. Another defeat, again on penalties, sent Portugal into the semi-finals, and reminded less credulous observers that England remained largely unproven.

'Not quite good enough' will serve as a summary of England's performances at World Cups. It has something to do with lack of high talent, but clearly not everything, as a team of honest players, firmly directed by manager and captain, triumphed in

1966. It has more to do with the culture of English football, which often resembles the Russian village that Potemkin designed for Catherine the Great. Players have been encouraged to think more highly of themselves than their skills warrant. It's disappointing, and don't expect it to change soon. Football at the highest level is not really an English game.

Introduction

Most people born in Lancashire enjoy their football, and I am no exception. For much of my early life I probably took more of an interest than is healthy. At the age of five I was taken to Burnden Park, where Bolton Wanderers ended up when they stopped 'trotting', and for the next twenty years I was committed to the game in a way that, glimpsed from the sunlit uplands of encroaching middle age, seems rather quaint.

Did I really drive the length and breadth of the land to watch matches involving teams with whom I had no emotional connection? Indeed I did; nor was I alone. Football used to be like that. In the 'golden age' of English football the appearance of Tom Finney or Stanley Matthews could put 20,000 on the gate. In 1969, when Roger Hunt joined Bolton from Liverpool, 5,000 well-wishers tootled along the East Lancs Road to watch his debut.

Burnden was home to the Trotters until 1997, when they moved to the Reebok Stadium, which is closer to Chorley than Bolton. Lowry depicted the ground in 'Going to the Match', so it survives on canvas, as it does in the imagination of all who knew it in the good old, bad old days. It was a decrepit place, as were so many of those grounds, yet it conveyed a flavour of

English football, with its wintry fug of brown ale, meat pies and Woodbines, more authentically than the clean lines of stadiums like the Reebok.

Going to the match! We would get there in good time, my father and I, buying a programme on the way in – a most important ritual – and Dad would be familiar with every player on both sides before kick-off. Week by week I digested everything he told me. 'Hull play in amber, not gold. Wolves play in gold. A great club, Wolves. Billy Wright played for them. Captain of England. But the most famous club is Arsenal. Bolton never beat them.' This was quite true. Arsenal came to Burnden in 1967, for a fourth-round FA Cup tie, and our hopes were high, but Bolton did not beat them.

Then the players would run out, solid men with proper names: Eddie Hopkinson, the goalie who had played for England, Syd Farrimond, John Hulme, Dave Lennard, John Byrom. The manager was Bill Ridding, promoted *faute de mieux* from the physiotherapist's room. It's easy to laugh at the way things used to be done, but funnier things have happened in our supposedly more progressive times. In 2008, facing a desperate fight against relegation, Newcastle United appointed Joe Kinnear.

Those years heard the last melancholy roar of the old order. Other than the Trotters, who won the FA Cup in 1958, Blackburn Rovers, Burnley and Preston North End all reached Wembley in the years between Suez and the 'white heat' of Harold Wilson's first government. Lancashire was the natural home of English football. To one mind it still is. Though I spend more time in

Berlin and Vienna these days than the county of my birth I am an unrepentant Red Rose nationalist where football is concerned. Like dubbined boots, players lining up in numbers 1 to 11, and matches kicking off at three o'clock on Saturday afternoon (and ending no later than 4.42), it is part of my personal mythology.

We are all prisoners of the past, and my love of football was forged on that old-fashioned ground. I may not have seen Nat Lofthouse, the great centre forward ennobled as the Lion of Vienna, but there were plenty of tales to stimulate my curiosity. My maternal grandfather had attended the 'White Horse' Cup Final of 1923, when the Wanderers beat West Ham United 2–0, and my mother was at Wembley for the so-called 'Matthews Final' thirty years later, when Blackpool came from behind to win 4–3, though she never cared for that sobriquet. 'It was Ernie Taylor who won it,' she used to say, 'not Matthews at all.' Actually, it was Stan Mortensen, who scored three goals that day: the hat-trick that nobody remembers!

In between those famous finals my parents had stood, separately, in a crowd of 84,000 (allegedly) at Burnden in March 1946 when thirty-three spectators were crushed to death during the match against Stoke City. Donny Davies, the celebrated football writer known to readers of the *Manchester Guardian* as 'Old International', who was to perish in English football's next tragedy, the Munich air crash of February 1958, was a friend of the family.

I mention these things to supply a context. If I now dislike so much about football, and what it has come to represent in our flattened national culture, it is painful, for the game gave me so much. Like thousands of others brought up in towns where Association Football played a full part in the life of what could still be called a community, I absorbed it naturally. There was no patronising talk of the game being part of 'popular culture'. That was implicit in our daily experience.

Francis Lee, the barrel-chested No. 7, was my hero, so when he left Bolton for Manchester City in October 1967 I followed him to Maine Road. Within seven months City were champions, with Lee their standard-bearer. Nine years later, at school by 'the staid and silver Trent', I observed the last knockings of his career at Derby County. I sent him one of only two fan letters I have ever written, and received a generous reply. When we eventually met, in 2003, I learned it had come from his hand.

'It was a lovely letter.'

'Course it was. I wrote it myself.'

'I thought secretaries did that kind of thing.'

'Don't talk daft.'

The other fan letter, incidentally, went to Bryan Ferry, who also replied in person: 'I have a new single coming out next month, called "The In Crowd". I hope you will like it.' Not every young boy is so lucky with his heroes.

At twelve, having passed the Common Entrance exam, my father gave me a copy of Arthur Hopcraft's book, *The Football Man*, which should require no amplification for anybody who loves the game. That path led to journalists such as Eric Todd, Hugh McIlvanney and David Lacey. But one man stood out. No England fixture was over until Brian Glanville had pronounced on it in the *Sunday Times*, with the command of an absolute monarch.

Through Glanville, with his understanding of the game not only in England but also in Europe and South America, it was possible to gain a wider perspective. He did for a curious young reader what Bernard Levin did in his very different columns: he opened doors. A fine life Glanville had. He had seen England win the World Cup in 1966 with a team of manly players and three all-time greats: Bobby Moore, Bobby Charlton and Gordon Banks. In 1970, they had an even stronger side. So did West Germany and, more significantly, so did Brazil. Despite England's quarter-final defeat at the hands of the Germans, when they surrendered a two-goal lead, that was a golden summer. It was the greatest World Cup there ever was, or will be.

Look at the photograph of Moore embracing Pelé after England had lost to Brazil, which has become one of the best-known images in sport. What you see, in a word, is joy: the joy of playing the game for something more than money or fame. For glory, as Danny Blanchflower said it should be played. No doubt some modern players have the same blood coursing through their veins, but none of Moore's successors is endowed with the natural dignity that people like to see in their sportsmen. For his breeding, as much as his talent, Moore was the greatest English footballer of my lifetime.

There is no joy in English football today, and little dignity. The game is richer, to the tune of many billions, yet it is poorer in spirit. The big grounds are full, but the bonds that yoked club to town or city have been sundered. Where clubs used to reflect civic pride, now they exist to make or – take a bow, Mike Ashley – lose money for the people who own them. Failure to win a trophy can bring public chastisement for even the best managers. When Arsene Wenger, who has transformed Arsenal into a side everybody loves to watch, is pilloried by Sid and Doris Bonkers, what hope is there for others?

For some judges, who have profited from the financial amplitude of the Premier League, life is a boon. Be grateful, groundlings! We're bringing the best players in the world to entertain you. For others, brought up to believe the game was never meant to be about gratuitous consumption, football has been disfigured. Many supporters no longer recognise it. The concentration of money, power and media interest in the top clubs has blocked their view.

Even the enthusiasts must blanch at the hysteria, racked up by ravenous media that demand 'excitement', and will happily simulate it where none exists. For all the money generated by the Premier League, and Sky Television, in international terms England remains a country of the second rank. Three times since 1966 the national side has failed to qualify for the World Cup, yet repeated failure has done nothing to diminish our sense of self-worth.

Off the field the game is run abysmally. The redevelopment of Wembley Stadium was an expensive shambles. The National Football Centre at Burton-on-Trent remains a work in progress. The Football Association may talk about 'respect' for referees but the failure to support officials, or punish the players who abuse them every week, is a badge of shame. There is no adherence to principle, only expediency.

There probably never was a truly blessed time for English football; no walk to the paradise garden. Grounds were shabby, and pitches could be heavy. Players were treated like serfs, and some of the tackling amounted to licensed thuggery. In some ways the game has improved. Few managers have been more committed to 'pure' football than Wenger, and there haven't been many better managers than Sir Alex Ferguson, who has turned out a succession of outstanding teams at Old Trafford.

Ferguson does not appear in this gallery. Despite his bullying of officials, a shortcoming that afflicts so many of his fellows, the Manchester United manager is healthily in credit when it comes to any assessment of his life's work. Consider the long, rich careers of Gary Neville, Paul Scholes and Ryan Giggs, or the reformation of Eric Cantona when it seemed that the Frenchman, having booted a lippy spectator at Crystal Palace, had forfeited any right to a second chance. No, Ferguson has not fouled up football.

Nor is Brian Clough on this list. He may have taken money out of the game but his teams never cheated. Any book of this sort carries the stamp of its author, and I am a fan of Clough, no matter what has been alleged. He liberated players and in doing so, he served football, and the people who watch it.

In other ways, things have not improved. Too many players show little respect for a game that rewards them so freely. Television and radio take the pampered badge-kissers at their own estimation; newspapers bump up every minor incident or disagreement. The perspective that Glanville offered readers is lost on some younger reporters, for whom every goal is 'sublime', every mistake 'tragic', every opportunity 'a final shot at redemption', and every second-rater who kicked a ball in anger, at whatever level, 'a club legend'.

As for the agents, who have redrawn the game's boundaries, many are beholden to none, and it shows. To borrow Mort Sahl's ringing phrase about the film director, Oliver Stone, they're the sort of people 'who describe accidents to witnesses'.

Society has become coarser in almost every respect, and social changes affect the games we play. One cannot hold football to account for all society's ills. That would be silly. But it is undeniable that, viewed from the outside, the game has an unrivalled capacity for infecting everything it touches, which is why this book holds to account some people who are not directly involved. As well as players, managers and owners there are administrators, agents, media personalities, referees, politicians, pop singers, film-makers and celebrity fans. Some are rotters; others are merely misguided. Yet they travel willingly on the same bus.

Uniquely among games, football exalts strident ignorance as the height of nobility. The tongue-tied international and the disgruntled supporter have become comic characters, but stupidity isn't funny. Only in English football would a player be regarded with suspicion by his own team-mates because he read a broadsheet newspaper. That is what happened to Graeme le Saux, a thoughtful man, whose paper of choice was the *Guardian*. More footballers should take the *Guardian*, if only to find out what Lacey has to say.

The football-foulers have forgotten – if, in some cases, they ever knew – that football is only a game; a great one, but ultimately only one among many. It is not a national pageant, or an alternative to life. 'I sometimes feel', John Arlott, the great cricket commentator, once said, 'that we are in danger of taking sport too seriously, and life not seriously enough.'

One stormy night in November 1985, I took wine with Arlott at his island retreat in Alderney. He spoke of old Hampshire cricketers, Thomas Hardy (Arlott had a full set of original editions), Louis MacNeice and E.M. Forster, who were colleagues from his BBC days, and Dylan Thomas, his one-time house-mate and 'the only man I ever kissed smack on the lips'. He loved Ian Botham, too; indeed, had taken the young man under his wing when others saw only trouble. Botham repaid the debt two decades later when he bought a house in Alderney, to be near his benefactor. Arlott would ring each morning, to invite him round for lunch, with the injunction: 'Bring your thirst with you!'

Three bottles in we got on to football. He had given up covering the game, he said, because it had become 'seedy'. It was no longer worth his while to spend Saturdays in places he no longer wanted to be. He had even been threatened by hooligans on a train. 'There are good people in the game,' he said, finding warm words for Joe Mercer and Ted Bates, the former Southampton manager. 'But remember, they are outnumbered about two hundred to one.'

Whether or not one agrees with Arlott, his words bore the authentic tone of a man who had witnessed the corruption of something he once loved. It wasn't age. He spoke with affection of many other things that had retained his love. Football had changed, and he didn't like those changes.

Like Arlott, I used to cover football. In two decades I reported from more than ninety Football League grounds, and it would be wrong to pretend that life was always miserable. Trips to Old Trafford and Anfield usually brought rewards, and you generally saw a good game at Nottingham Forest and Ipswich Town. But in time I too grew tired of the excesses, the lies, the equivocations.

Football has been shamed by people who do not hold its best interests at heart. Too few love it as a game should be loved, with affection balanced by the critical detachment one must apply to all things that are worth doing. This may be an indignant book but, as George Sand wrote, indignation is the highest form of love.

1 Roman Abramovich

The Russians have always had a strange relationship with Europe. A Slavic race by geography and temperament, they have both feared the West and sought Western approval, or at least recognition.

Peter the Great made St Petersburg his 'window to the West', but the Enlightenment he sought to embrace did not touch Russia, which preferred then, as now, to look inward. Their sorely tried people have never enjoyed the fruits of democracy, and never will. Holy Mother Russia must therefore find its strength in other ways. Tolstoy and Dostoevsky wrote endlessly about the sanctity of Russian soil, and the holiness of the Russian soul. At Boris Pasternak's funeral in 1960 mourners who had been forbidden to read his poems in print were able to recite them from memory.

Such is the emotional bond between the Russians and their writers, who have always been the nation's true representatives. Their composers, ladling out double helpings of romantic gloom like tubs of ginger pudding, also speak a recognisable language. The struggle makes for great art but the cost in human terms has been enormous. Sometimes, as in the case of Shostakovich, it is unimaginable. These people are not like us. They are not like anybody.

The cliché of the Russian exile who weeps at the thought of a birch tree is not misplaced. Through the centuries Russia has lost its best and brightest, who have not been able to live in their own land, yet who have been unable to shake off their ancestry. This was particularly strong in the early decades of the twentieth century when Sergei Diaghilev and the Ballets Russes conquered Paris, with Igor Stravinsky as house composer. Stravinsky, who lived in France, Switzerland and America, admitted, on visiting his native land towards the end of his days, that he had never escaped the Russian landscape.

Who does Russia send us now? Which people follow in the footsteps of Diaghilev and Stravinsky? Rich and vulgar people, that's who. People like Roman Abramovich. With five boats, including the world's biggest yacht, the 557-foot *Eclipse*, built in Hamburg for £330 million, complete with a missile-detection system, and a portfolio of expensive properties across the world, including a fortress-mansion in Belgravia, Abramovich has become the most visible symbol of the Russian billionaire.

Those yachts often come in handy. In August 2008 his party was refused service at a restaurant on the coast of Tuscany. While it was unclear whether or not the restaurant was full, it was abundantly plain that Italians have had enough of rich, bumptious Russians. 'Try again tomorrow,' the restaurant manager told Abramovich, who promptly ordered his yacht to Sardinia.

Two things distinguish him from the pack. He is Jewish, which, in a traditionally anti-Semitic country like Russia, is enough to make him stand out. And he owns a football club,

Chelsea, which has given him an international profile denied
to those Russians who have stayed at home. He has also spent
£60 million on two paintings, by Francis Bacon and Lucian
Freud, reportedly on the advice of his girlfriend, one Daria
Zhukova, who has opened a gallery in Moscow. When she was
asked which painters she liked, Miss Zhukova was reported to
have replied: 'I'm, like, really bad at remembering names.'

Born in Siberia, orphaned at four, Abramovich made his
billions in the plunder of oil reserves after the collapse of
communism in the old Soviet Union. In the free-for-all that
went on, sanctioned by officials, he was able to acquire a
shareholding that was eventually worth billions. At the height
of his prosperity he was reckoned to be worth £23 billion.

Abramovich caught the football bug, it is said, when he
watched Real Madrid's demolition of Manchester United at Old
Trafford in 2003. Within a year he had bought Chelsea for £150
million, and at once began to bankroll the club to the Premier
League, which they won twice in succession, and then the
Champions League. After a series of disappointments, not always
taken gracefully, they came within a penalty kick of becoming
European champions in 2008, in Moscow, where their owner
had planned a Boris Godunov-like coronation for his
homecoming.

Chelsea's swaggering style, developed before Abramovich's
arrival, was not to all tastes. Once he had arrived, moneybags
on his saddle, pistols blazing, the swaggering intensified. Chelsea
spent millions acquiring players, some of whom were discarded
at will. It brought them those championships under Jose

Mourinho, the Portuguese coach, but at the cost of public affection. Neutrals admired a player like Gianfranco Zola, who brought a winning personality as well as high skill. They did not admire some of the players who, seduced by Russian money, followed the Italian to Stamford Bridge.

It is never easy to warm to outsiders who run up debts in order to satisfy their own whim. In 2008 Mr Justice Christopher Clarke described Abramovich's involvement with Chelsea as 'a hobby and a leisure interest'. That year Abramovich usually spent a day and a half at a time in England. His longest stay was eleven days, in which he attended four Chelsea matches, watching from the comfort of a private box.

Chelsea's rise to the top of the Premier League was accompanied by a lack of dignity that was breathtaking in its candour. At the heart of it was the billionaire owner, who would burst into the dressing-room to celebrate with the players, or remonstrate with the managers. One player, Andriy Shevchenko, from Ukraine, was expressly brought in to satisfy the owner's whim, and failed so miserably that he was shipped back to Milan, his former club, on loan. In this clash of wills with Mourinho there could be only one winner, and soon Mourinho was off, eventually to Milan, where he took Internazionale to a championship title that proved beyond his successors at Chelsea.

If his departure was a grubby affair, and the promotion and subsequent dismissal of Avram Grant were bewildering, the recruitment and sacking of Felipe Scolari were astounding. The Brazilian, a World Cup-winning manager, no less, was fired after eight months because he had not come up to scratch. It was the behaviour of a tetchy man used to getting his own way, and Guus Hiddinck's FA Cup triumph that followed Scolari's departure did nothing to gainsay it.

Abramovich has brought wealth to London, and has had the vulgarity to splash it. His money has been good for Chelsea, not nearly so good for English football. When the day dawns, as it surely will, to spend his billions in the art world, on works by painters his girlfriend has never heard of, he will leave with everybody's blessing.

2 Sam Allardyce

Here's a thought to quicken the pulse. Imagine, when Sven-Goran Eriksson stepped aside as England manager, that the Football Association had invited 'Big' Sam Allardyce to succeed him. He might have been better than Steve McClaren, did you say? Very well. Let us measure the ways.

Football, first. Bolton Wanderers played some lovely stuff on his watch. Their passing and movement delighted all who watched them. Didn't the arrival in your parish of Sam's Trotters put a spring in everybody's step on the way to the ground? Did you not hear people say: 'We're bound to savour a feast of football today'? No fibbing now.

Next, the man. When Alan Green, one of the few people whose pulse did not quicken at the prospect of watching Bolton, called their football 'ugly', Allardyce banned him from the Reebok Stadium. It isn't easy to warm to Green, but radio commentators are entitled to hold honest opinions. To ban a reporter for failing to fall into line is the mark of a very small man indeed, no matter what Allardyce's pet name suggests.

Never knowingly funny, he can make the crustiest of High Court judges laugh when he gets on his high horse. Adopting

his more-in-sorrow-than-anger face, and affecting the peeved tones of an alderman who has been taken for a plumber, he regularly tells television viewers how 'disappointed' he is with referees' decisions. BBC viewers are spared his thoughts. He has not spoken to the corporation since *Panorama* shone a critical spotlight on the commercial activities of Craig, his agent son.

By not speaking to the main national broadcaster he is following the example of his pal, Sir Alex Ferguson. Indeed, there are times when Allardyce appears to be Ferguson's amanuensis. He seems so keen to take Ferguson's side that at times he sounds like the verger in *Dad's Army*, forever backing up Bill Pertwee's pedantic ARP warden against Captain Mainwaring. As England manager, however, Allardyce would have had to speak to the corporation.

'Big Sam', as he is called by people who affect a puzzling familiarity, was hurt not to have got the nod. Was he not the very model of a modern football manager? Players could hardly move at the Reebok without bumping into a nutritionist or psychologist. But, like so many football folk, he bridles when people find less merit in his management than he does.

It has not been a bad career. By recruiting sensibly, mainly from overseas, he kept Bolton in the Premier League and took them into the Uefa Cup. After a brief interlude at Newcastle United, where he was denied a proper chance to strut and fret his hour upon a bigger stage, he slipped snugly into the manager's seat at Blackburn Rovers when Paul Ince was dismissed. If Ince had stayed in charge, Blackburn would almost certainly have been relegated. With Allardyce at the helm they stayed up. He knows his way around, 'Big Sam'. He's a trouper.

In small ways, though, he shows his colours. When Morten Gamst Pedersen, Blackburn's Norwegian midfielder, was publicly humiliated for a hilarious dive at Arsenal, bringing guffaws from a television audience, Allardyce unburdened himself in a way that revealed rather more than he might have wanted people to know.

You might think that, by diving, or committing acts of 'simulation', a weasel word that disguises true meaning, players are subverting the game, and should therefore be named and shamed. You might go further, and say that managers who offer public support for the worst offenders, or who fail to punish them, are guilty of complicity. Yet managers will never find fault with their own players so long as there are others to blame, usually the referee.

Allardyce's response to Pedersen's dive was curious, to say the least. 'Until Keith Hackett (the FA referees assessor) decides that fouls should be given for players who manage to stay on their feet,' he said, 'then people will always cheat.' Dirty players should be booked, he said, so that others 'would not need to resort to diving'.

There is logic of a kind in his summary, but it is logic that leads to the madhouse. Note the verb, 'resort' to diving. Managers conjugate the verb thus: my players resort to diving, yours go to ground early, theirs cheat. So let's all cheat, and then blame the refs!

Allardyce is not the only manager to consider events

selectively. But, by seeking to deflect blame from his own player, who was clearly in the wrong, he exposed the woolliness of so much managerial thinking. Far from protecting the integrity of the game, too many managers undermine it because they will not offer the wholehearted support that officials need.

Were they to make it plain that they would not tolerate play-acting of any kind, to the extent of dropping persistent offenders who 'resorted', poor mites, to acts of deception, they would provide a notable service. Instead they opt to bully referees, who make easy targets because they make mistakes – though many fewer than most managers and players. Bill Nicholson, the great Tottenham manager, liked to remind his men of that unwritten law before they left the dressing-room. His successors, fearing a backlash from players who are a thousand times richer, and therefore less likely to listen, are more mealy-mouthed.

Perhaps, like cricketers, footballers should return to the middle after they retire, to apply the knowledge they acquired in their playing days as decision-makers. Until more of them do, it is hard to take seriously those moaning minnies who calumniate match officials for lacking 'consistency', a quality which, of course, shines out of every manager's ears. That would take humility, and humility doesn't win you many points.

Primitive football, pettiness, buck-passing. Perhaps it's best not to imagine 'Big Sam' as the figurehead of English football. It would have been a return to the Dark Ages.

3 Mike Ashley

It is impossible to imagine a more spectacular own goal than Mike Ashley's wanton destruction of Newcastle United. In two years of curious decisions, followed by occasional acts of repentance, the sportswear tycoon brought the club to its knees. When relegation from the Premier League came in May 2009, it capped twenty-two months of unstinting efforts by an owner who seemed to have no idea what he had bought.

When Ashley arrived in July 2007 he enjoyed the goodwill of supporters, who had tired of the previous owners. The Hall and Shepherd families had enriched themselves to the tune of £145 million through salaries, dividends and sales of shares, and people were happy to overlook the fact that Ashley was an outsider, a Home Counties lad who supported Tottenham. Had he not bought Newcastle for £135 million, cleared debts of £43 million and given the club an interest-free loan of £100 million? He had, and he was made most welcome.

He began to attract attention, it is true, when he attended matches wearing a replica shirt. This act of brazen populism did not play well beyond Newcastle, and there were plenty of people within the city walls who thought little of this showboating. Ashley was, after all, representing the club, not auditioning for the big top. There were also stories about picking up the tab when he visited a local bar. It is not something that Viscount Westwood, one of the Ashley's predecessors, and a chairman of the Football Association, would have countenanced.

Still, Ashley's reputation survived the sacking of Sam Allardyce, whose appointment he had inherited, in January 2008. And when he invited Kevin Keegan to return to St James' Park, and took to wearing a replica shirt that proclaimed 'King Kev', his populist instincts helped allay the fears of those fans who sensed that something rum was going on.

Not for long. When the storm broke everybody got soaked. To assist Keegan in his attempts to reshape the club Ashley brought in Chris Mort, a London solicitor, as chairman. Derek Llambias, a casino director, joined the club as managing director, and there was a mind-boggling overhaul of the football side, which saw the recruitment of what proved to be an unholy trinity.

At the top of it was Denis Wise, an unsavoury character who had been convicted, when a Chelsea player, of assaulting a London cab driver, and who was sacked by Leicester City after assaulting a team-mate, Callum Davidson. Wise had just stood down as manager of Leeds United when Ashley pounced, and the grounds for his appointment were unclear, as his record in eighteen months at Leeds revealed that he had taken them down, and then appeared to lose interest in management.

Nevertheless Wise was given the title 'executive director (football)', a fancy way of describing somebody whose duties meant that he could continue to live near London, and scour the Continent for half-decent players. It didn't take Keegan long to question this arrangement, particularly when he found that his own judgement of players was considered inadequate. In September 2008, soured by the sale of James Milner to Aston Villa against his wishes, Keegan walked out.

That still left Wise in situ, holding hands with the other members of the peculiar trio. Jeff Vetere was the 'technical coordinator', another fuzzy description, and Tony Jimenez was a vice-president responsible for the recruitment of players. Crucially Jimenez was pally with Paul Kemsley, the former vice-chairman of Tottenham, and a good friend of Ashley's. It didn't take long for the fans to dub them the 'cockney mafia', and, once dubbed, the term stuck.

An executive director who lived 300 miles away, a technical co-ordinator, and a vice-president with a bulging contacts book: this was what Newcastle had been reduced to in the autumn of 2008. All Ashley needed to make a complete botch of the job was a manager dredged from the back of beyond. As if on cue Joe Kinnear walked through the door.

Kinnear was a rank outsider, a man who made a reputation of sorts as a combative manager of Wimbledon, but whose last involvement with the game had been a brief, inglorious stay at Nottingham Forest in 2004. Locals did not take to another Londoner, and they took to Kinnear even less when he swore fifty times, like a disturbed teenager, at journalists during his first press conference.

Ashley, aware of the turning of the tide, put the club up for sale, but nobody would bite. The team's abysmal form meant that putative buyers wanted to see how Newcastle would end the season. The arrival of Alan Shearer as caretaker manager, when Kinnear stood down to have a heart bypass operation, renewed public interest, for Shearer was a local man, and a distinguished former player: the club's record goalscorer, no less. But even he couldn't prevent their relegation, which was confirmed on the final day of the season at Aston Villa.

Wise had gone by then, leaving on 1 April, as if to prove the whole thing had been a joke in poor taste. The players he brought to the club were moved on as Newcastle prepared for life outside the Premier League. To general hilarity, except on Tyneside, where disgust had given way to resignation, he renamed their famous home 'sportsdirect.com@StJames'Park stadium'.

Ashley made £929 million when he floated his company, Sports Direct International, on the Stock Exchange. The deal made him feel like a king, and kings like to assemble a court around them. Ashley's court at Newcastle was reduced to a rabble in a matter of months, leaving him with a tatty crown and a broken reputation. In its singular way it was a notable achievement. Not everybody can say they played the king and the fool in one lifetime.

4 David Baddiel

English humour is a difficult code for foreigners to crack. As a people we value irony, sarcasm, wordplay, punning, understatement and self-deprecation, sometimes to excess. It can be quirky, and it can be mannered. Eccentricity is not always loveable; many would-be eccentrics try too hard to acquire a quality that can only arise naturally. As for 'zany', it is a handy signpost: usually it points to somebody who is monumentally unfunny.

Think of the comedians who capture something of this English spirit, and certain names spring to mind: Ken Dodd, Frankie Howerd, Eric Morecambe, Tommy Cooper, Les Dawson. There are anecdotalists, like Kenneth Williams, comic actors, like Ronnie Barker, and the occasional anarchist, like Spike Milligan. Victoria Wood has earned the right to join the club. David Baddiel hasn't.

In recent years there has been a distortion of traditional comic standards. You can sense it in the altered vocabulary of critics who admire 'subversion', our old friend 'irreverence' (which translates as ostentatious rudeness) and – yes, they really mean it – 'post-modern irony'. What follows is not bawdy but aggression. Or, in Baddiel's case, insufferable smugness.

The rot set in, one could argue, with Peter Cook, the star of *Beyond the Fringe*, the hit of the 1960 Edinburgh Festival which also featured Alan Bennett, Jonathan Miller and Dudley Moore. The show went from Edinburgh to the West End, and then to Broadway, where it was garlanded with honours, and should have set up Cook for life. Alas, he hit the bottle, and was never as sharp again, though he was never short of friends who liked to tell the world how amusing he was.

Hugh Leonard, the Irish playwright, made an interesting distinction: Bennett's talent went to his brain, Cook's to his head. In that respect he was the first modern comedian. He laughed at his own jokes, even if nobody else did, because he thought he knew better than they. Some of his jokes were good, for he was funny, but his attitude revealed an insolence that is less attractive in those, not nearly so gifted, who have followed.

Late in his life, addled by booze, a mere shadow of the man who delighted so many, Cook was routed on live television by Bernard Manning. 'You were funny tonight, Peter,' goaded Manning, looking for a confrontation he was denied. Cook, afraid to take on an adversary of Manning's low cunning, sat there and took it.

Looking around the altered world of comedy, when music hall and variety have given way to a parade of young shavers falling over each other to secure television deals, can be pretty dispiriting. How, one wonders, did Baddiel ever find a stage to play on? A clever-clogs north Londoner, who took a double first in English at Cambridge, Baddiel has a face that never quite manages to conceal immense self-satisfaction. When he landed a presenter's role on BBC Television's *Fantasy Football League*, in partnership with his former lodger, Frank Skinner, he preened himself like a dog with four testicles.

For a certain sort of football fan, familiar with the world of fanzines and alternative comedy, *Fantasy Football League* represented something weird and wonderful. Audiences were encouraged to turn up for each show wearing their club colours, to offer an illusion of harmony. If they were good they were rewarded at curtain-down time with a song from Jeff Astle, the former centre forward for West Bromwich Albion, Skinner's club. At least Angus 'Statto' Loughran, on hand to supply relevant facts, had the grace to look as if he had wandered into the wrong studio.

Fortified by strong drink, many people were amused by this late-night divertissement. Many, but not all. Jimmy Greaves and Ian St John, television performers of a different hue, did not take kindly to being mocked when they were invited on to the show. Here were two players of the recent past, one a true great, the other a very-good, being used for knockabout material by a mid-ranking end-of-pier act. Whether it was post-modern irony or a simple lack of respect, it spelt out an unmistakeable message: we're a couple of swells.

The European Championship of 1996 was supposed to be their finest hour. Baddiel and Skinner wrote the words to a tune by a pop group called the Lightning Seeds, and in no time 'Football's Coming Home', with its line about 'thirty years of hurt', became the tournament's much-hummed theme song. Elevated to performer status, the pier-enders turned up in the royal box at Wembley to lead the sing-along.

It was too good to last. The final image of England's partici-pation in that championship was of Baddiel, standing where Her Majesty sits, ready to take Wembley's salute, looking on in dismay as England lost the semi-final to Germany on penalties. Football wasn't coming home after all. What a swizz! Those three barren decades would stretch into a fourth, and a fifth.

In May 2009, when England launched their bid to stage the 2018 World Cup, it was agreed that 'football's coming home', far from boosting their chances of landing the tournament, would play into the hands of their rivals, so it was gently dropped. Baddiel, who knows his Shakespeare, was hoist with his own petard. Like many among the new breed of comics, he had tilted his lance at the evils of sexism, racism, this-ism, that-ism, yet his song of homecoming eventually came to be known as a tribute to John Bull.

And thus the whirligig of time brings in his revenges.

5 Tony Banks

Arnold Bennett had a word for it. 'A card', he called Denry Machin, the hero of his well-known novel. When somebody asked, 'What great cause is he identified with?', the answer was swift: 'With the great cause of cheering us all up.'

Such folk must be cherished. Even in the Palace of Westminster some people are licensed to wear the jester's cap and bells, to divert others from the serious business of government. So long as they know their bounds they are welcome; the trick is to tread carefully. Tony Banks made the mistake of thinking he was one of life's natural comedians, and paid the price. By the time he died at the age of sixty-four the bringer of occasional mirth had become a figure of fun.

It is not all that difficult to play the cheeky chappie in the House of Commons. Undermining the solemnity of political debate by blowing a raspberry or two in the guise of the common man is within the reach of many MPs, and Banks had a grasp of the demotic, if nothing else. When he was called to office, he found it hard to put away childish things, so he made a poor Minister of Sport. Comics never look completely happy in a collar and tie.

Appointed Minister of Sport in Tony Blair's first, bright-as-day administration, Banks the republican Chelsea fan declined to watch the 1998 Cup Final from the royal box – 'in case it spoiled my enjoyment', as he graciously put it. Having realised his blunder, the Prime Minister shifted him to another role, 'special envoy' to England's World Cup bid. The change of responsibilities did not suit this resolute against-the-tider.

Charged with leading the fight to bring the World Cup to England in 2006, Banks played his hand so poorly that the Germans came from behind to win, as they do so often on the field. Politics, it is said, is the art of the possible. But things are possible only if politicians demonstrate a tact and adroitness that enable them to be taken seriously. Nobody ever took Banks as seriously as he took himself in a role for which he was unsuited by temperament or talent. As they say in the opera world, of singers who find roles too taxing, he was overparted.

To be fair, he inherited an awkward situation. By bidding for the World Cup the Football Association had reneged on a gentleman's agreement with the Germans that they would support their World Cup bid in exchange for German endorsement of a European Championship in England in 1996. That volte-face did little to impress other members, who felt that the nation which invented the idea of fair play had not, in this instance, lived up to its reputation.

Nor did it help Banks that, in Franz Beckenbauer, Germany had the best possible advocate. Not only had he led the Germans to one World Cup as captain in 1974, and to another as manager sixteen years later, he was also a superb performer in the corridors of diplomacy. He was an ambassador. Like many Germans, he spoke the English language better than most native speakers; better, whisper it, than the British envoy.

A combative man, Banks was intolerant when the criticism was returned. He made himself look petty when he abused Mihir Bose, the investigative reporter, in front of a bemused Beckenbauer. Politicians must expect scrutiny, particularly when the nation is trying to host an international tournament like a World Cup, and Banks revealed a very thin skin when Bose began to ask the probing questions that most politicians learn to play with the deadest of bats.

But he also fouled up football in another significant way. Manchester United won the FA Cup in their 'treble' year of 1999 but, so great was the pressure applied on them by the Football Association, which was obsessed by the World Cup bid, that they withdrew from the following season's competition. It was a scandal then, and the intervening years have done nothing to diminish the shame.

By sending United to Brazil, to compete in the FIFA Club World Championship in January 2000, the Football Association, backed by the government, were agents in the devaluation of their own tournament, which is the greatest knock-out cup in the whole of team sport. This was not exclusively Banks's fault but a cannier politician would have ensured that United defended their trophy, even if it meant sending out a reserve side until the first-choice players returned from Brazil. Instead he said their absence would cause 'irreparable damage' to England's chances of hosting the World Cup. It was a squalid episode which harmed the reputations of all who were touched by it. Not that it did him much harm. He got his peerage.

Lord Stratford was not terribly funny, not terribly bright and not terribly effective. Not much of a card at all.

6 Joey Barton

There's a lot to be said for belonging to the human race. Every day brings something to freshen the bloom. Trees, flowers, birds, the sound of water, the sky at night, music, paintings, books, wine, food, the company of friends, and a thousand other things that flesh is heir to. Whatever we make of it, life is good.

One of the few things to be said against it is a kinship with the likes of Joey Barton. Part-time footballer, full-time oik, Barton has the field to himself in any assessment of modern players who have earned a grubby crust.

The problem is simple: he chose the wrong sport. The game he should have taken up is rugby, which tends to sort out such people in a matter of hours. For rugby players, brought up on a physical game, where violence is never far away, the idea of football 'hard men' is a poor joke. How many would win a tickling contest with a warrior like Martin Johnson, or step on to the field to face the Springboks? Ladies and gentlemen of the jury, you may retire to complete your deliberations. It should not take long

Rugby players are not angels. They can behave badly at times, on and off the field. But how much more wholesome football would be if players tried to match the standards set by the men who play the fifteen-a-side code – and men is the appropriate noun. Too many footballers are boys who have been indulged in a world that pardons the cheat. Rugby players are expected to get on with it, without whingeing, or pointing the finger at opponents, unless those opponents are trying to gouge their eyes out. Most important of all, they accept the referee's word without contradiction. In that world, where bad 'uns are soon identified, young men tend to grow up fairly quickly.

When England's rugby players won the World Cup in 2003, beating Australia, the reigning champions, in Sydney, there was a moment, towards the end of extra time, which highlighted the difference in attitude between their game and football. Jonny Wilkinson, targeted for acts of aggression throughout the afternoon, had taken yet another ferocious tackle that left him winded. As he regained his breath not a single England player offered assistance.

Led by Johnson, a captain for whom the word indomitable might have been minted, they simply waited for their star goal-kicker to come round. To have made a fuss of Wilkinson was not their style. It generally isn't with rugby players. They are hard men, who do not expect sympathy when they are on the wrong end of rough play. The rest we know. Wilkinson, having recovered, kicked his team to a famous victory.

A thug like Barton would have lasted no longer than a week in rugby. A man who tries to settle every dispute with his fists, as Barton does, would have been sent home with a cracked crown to reflect on the folly of his ways. Instead this violent, disturbed man has been offered so many second chances that the game has been defiled by his presence. It's not as if he's a good player. Judged by the standards to which he aspires, he's pretty ordinary.

The charge-sheet is long and gruesome. In 2004, as a Manchester City player, he put a cigar into the eyes of Jamie Tandy, an apprentice, at the club's Christmas party. At the end of that season, on a trip to Thailand, he assaulted an Everton supporter in a bar. He could have been dismissed for either of those offences. The club merely fined him, and issued a warning about his behaviour.

As anybody could have told them, there would be no reformation. In 2007 Barton punched Ousmane Dabo, a team-mate, in an argument at the training ground that left the Frenchman unconscious, nursing a broken cheekbone. The astonishing aspect of this revolting episode (Barton attacked his victim from behind) was that none of the other players intervened on Dabo's behalf. When the case came to court in July 2008 Barton received a four-month suspended sentence after he admitted occasioning actual bodily harm. Two months earlier he had been handed a six-month prison sentence, after being convicted of common assault and affray in a Liverpool street, but served only seventy-seven days.

By this time City had washed their hands of him, and he was a Newcastle United player. Kevin Keegan, Barton's manager in Manchester, had taken over at St James' Park and promised to stand by his man. The player was packed off to the Sporting Clinic in Hampshire, a place that tries to help those people who, to use the debased language of our times, have 'anger management issues'. They did their best. But some people are beyond help.

When he eventually returned to the north east, to join a team determined to be relegated, Barton was given a chance to remind everybody he was still a footballer. He repaid Alan Shearer, the new Newcastle manager, in a manner that was entirely typical, launching into a reckless challenge on Liverpool's Xavi Alonso at Anfield that brought instant dismissal and an immediate rebuke from Shearer, who called it 'a coward's tackle'.

When others might have spent a solemn hour in reflection Barton went on a verbal rampage. He told Shearer he was a 'shit manager', and informed the dressing-room that he, Joey Bighead, was the best player in the side. Shearer acted with commendable restraint. He made the player available for transfer, with the rejoinder: 'He won't take the piss out of this club, and he won't take the piss out of this city'.

Unable to master the flaws of his character, untainted by self-knowledge, this lout has taken football yobbery to new depths of infamy. The game also comes out of it badly. Managers who should have known better sought to 'understand' him, when a much stiffer response was required. In a decade of vile behaviour he has learned not a thing. Ten minutes on a rugby field would have saved us all the bother.

7 Ken Bates

A man with a white beard is usually a jolly chap. Captain Bird's Eye brought us those excellent fish fingers, George Bernard Shaw was forever chuckling at his own cleverness, and James Robertson Justice made a splendid doctor in the house. Then there is Santa Claus, who dispenses gifts to well-behaved children all over the world at Christmas, taking only a mince pie for his pains.

Ken Bates has a white beard, too, but nobody has ever mistaken him for Jolly Jack Falstaff. Not for him an evening of pranks in the tavern with Bardolph of the mighty conk, washed down with goblets of sack served by Mistress Quickly. No laundry basket ride into the Thames, though that is where many people within football would like to dunk him.

For the past four decades, as he has slipped in and out of four clubs, from Oldham to Leeds by way of Wigan and Chelsea, Master Bates of Monaco has presented a less generous face to the world, as though he holds a grudge that cannot possibly be assuaged. He shouldn't be too surprised, therefore, when people grind their teeth whenever he hoves into view. 'A footballing cretin', was Martin O'Neill's appraisal. He didn't meet much of an argument.

Others have been less kind. Having sold his shareholding in Chelsea to Roman Abramovich, in a move engineered by the master fixer, Pini Zahavi, Bates called the Israeli agent 'a dickhead'. Zahavi, who is not a man to rile, said: 'This revolting character is not worthy of a response. If I was in his shoes I would wake up every morning praying to God and thanking him that I saved him from bankruptcy and put £19 million in his pocket.' Seventeen million, actually, but Zahavi makes his point.

No man of God, Bates is familiar with the pulpit. In his heyday at Chelsea, the club he bought for £1 in 1982, he mounted it on most match days to denounce his enemies in colourful programme notes. Players, managers, administrators and journalists came alike to the man who was determined to inherit Carlyle's title as the Sage of Chelsea. Sometimes he saw foes within his own camp. Matthew Harding, Chelsea's vice-chairman, found himself banned from the boardroom, and Bates's plans to ring Stamford Bridge with an electric fence, to deter hooligans, were dashed by the Greater London Council.

One day his bumper bag of barbs was likely to land on his toe, and that day arrived in July 2009. Bates was the chairman of Leeds United by then, and had presided over one of the most lamentable chapters in the club's history as they slipped into the old Third Division in 2007, went into administration, were docked fifteen points for breaching Football League insolvency rules, and had to be reconstituted by a network of offshore companies.

Astor Investments, a Guernsey-based trust fund, agreed to write off £17.6 million of debt so long as Bates remained chairman of the new club, so he still had some friends, even if it wasn't clear who they were. The identity of Bates's backers has always been a mystery.

His restoration did not still his busy quill. Bates launched three attacks in match-day programmes on Melvyn Levi, a former Leeds director, who had belonged to the consortium of businessmen who ran the club before Bates arrived in 2005. Levi, Bates wrote, was 'a shyster' trying to 'blackmail' the club. When Levi sued for libel the High Court found in his favour, awarding him £50,000, and making Bates liable for all costs, estimated at £1.5 million. The judge, Sir Charles Gray, referred to the 'gratuitous inclusion' of Levi's address in the match programme.

Among Leeds fans, who had never taken to Bates and his secretive ways, the view was that it couldn't have happened to a nicer chap. Within the game at large no tears were shed. Kate Hoey, the Minister for Sport when Bates was bulldozing through plans for a new Wembley Stadium, spoke for many when she called him 'a bully'.

His attempts to bully the Football League into reversing their fifteen-point deduction failed abysmally. Having heard his call for Lord Mawhinney, the League chairman, to be fired, for observing the rules designed to bind all clubs, they decided that the punishment should stand. When Leeds reached the play-off final at Wembley in 2008, Bates solemnly informed the press that, even with the noble lord in attendance, he would behave. In the event Doncaster Rovers won the match, and Bates looked on like a Roman emperor who had backed the wrong chariot.

At least he had returned to Wembley, the stadium he had helped to rebuild. Bates cannot be held accountable for the appalling delays in completing the work, nor the constant extension of the budget. But his enthusiasm for the project, as chairman of Wembley National Stadium Ltd, will not be forgotten by football supporters who felt, not unreasonably, that a new national stadium could have been constructed in the Midlands or the North at a fraction of the cost. Without the twin towers, those symbols of place and history, the modernised Wembley is a functional, charmless, corporate place.

Why, you may wonder, does a man in his eighth decade carry on? It can't be love of a particular club. He's had four of them. It can't be love of the game and those in it. People loathe him. Perhaps it is the thrill of confrontation, which makes his world go round. But when you are the chairman of a Third Division club, people don't want to confront you. They just ignore you.

Bates may have a white beard. But don't leave a mince pie out for him on Christmas Eve. He'll only flog it.

8 Victoria Beckham

The cult of David Beckham is one of the most perplexing features of modern life. A good footballer, far from being the best of his generation, has achieved a degree of notoriety that goes so far beyond the world of sport that he may be regarded as a global phenomenon.

That it is a commercial, as opposed to sporting, phenomenon is beyond argument. As a footballer he is not in the same street as Paul Scholes, his former team-mate at Manchester United. He is not in the same city as Paolo Maldini, whom he joined at Milan. He is not in the same time zone as Zinedine Zidane, with whom he played with at Real Madrid, on those occasions that Beckham managed to get a game. Maldini and Zidane achieved a greatness of which Beckham can only dream.

Yet it is his name that appeared in the title of a hit film, and which Madrid, the world's most famous football club, recruited to sell replica shirts in the overseas market. When London accepted the baton from Peking to host the 2012 Olympics, it was 'Becks' who was wheeled out to boot a football into the crowd. The Football Association, anxious to bring the World Cup to England in 2018, appointed him as one of their

ambassadors. He helped bring down the curtain on Michael Parkinson's final talk show.

When he eventually won his hundredth international cap, a target he had very consciously set himself, Beckham joined a club that contained only four other members. But, whereas Billy Wright, Bobby Moore, Bobby Charlton and Peter Shilton belonged in the first rank of England players, Beckham could not be considered certain of a place in the second tier. Beckham-fever, it cannot be denied, is a most peculiar phenomenon.

At his best, playing for United in his twenties, he was very good. He couldn't head the ball, was a reluctant tackler, had no left foot to speak of, rarely beat a defender through change of pace, and didn't score many goals in open play. The other side of the ledger revealed an excellent right foot, which he used to play in strikers and provide first-class crosses from the right wing, provided his team-mates could engineer enough space. He took some fine free kicks, too.

Unlike Wright, Moore and Charlton, who were captains in deed as well as title, Beckham often behaved like an infant. He is the only man to have been sent off twice in an England shirt, and on both occasions his offences were unnecessary. Against Argentina in the 1998 World Cup he flicked out a leg to catch Diego Simone. Eight years later, captaining the side against Austria, he committed a silly foul moments after the referee had declined to give a free kick his way.

Is it too easy to say his career went into decline after he married Victoria Adams, a pop star? Yes, it is. Beckham was a model professional, who practised hard and never put himself above his peers at Old Trafford, where he remains popular. He made the most of what he had. Before his head was turned, and football interests took second place to brand recognition, it was easy to admire Beckham the pro.

But the values of the pop world he married into were bound to leave some kind of mark because they have more to do with marketing than talent. As John Giles, the former Leeds United and Ireland midfielder, said, publicity was oxygen for Mrs Beckham, cyanide for him.

His wife's rise to celebrity (one cannot call it fame, which implies achievement) is also an odd business. This mousy suburban Circe can neither sing nor dance very well, nor is she particularly attractive, yet she found celebrity as part of a girl group manufactured to titillate pre-pubescent boys; a kind of Monkees in reverse, with 'Posh Spice' playing the role of Micky Dolenz.

To go by everything she has said publicly in their years of marriage, Miss Adams appears to think dimness is a virtue. The marriage itself was a minor masterpiece of showbiz folderol, with an Irish castle hired for the occasion, the happy couple sitting on his-and-hers golden thrones, and exclusive picture rights granted to one of those magazines people flick through at the barbers. Greatly to their credit the Irish ignored this gaudy event, though there was one unintended comic moment when the pair commissioned a coat of arms, which had a swan gliding outwards, rather than inwards, as heraldic custom decrees. 'Who gives a shit?' was her tart response. Ah, the grace that launched a thousand ships.

Soon Beckham the one-time footballer was doing any number of daft things to keep his name before the public. He changed his barnet every month, and painted his body with odd symbols. He wore his wife's undies, and became a gay 'icon'. He posed, Christ-like, at Easter, for *Time Out*, the London listings magazine, though it wasn't clear he knew what Easter was. Mrs Beckham said they would like the children to be baptised, but weren't sure about the faith. And they wondered why people laughed.

As for the children's names, one feels for the dears. Brooklyn was bad enough, but Cruz and Romeo raised the bar another couple of notches. This is 'posh' as in fur coat, no knickers, not port out, starboard home. They can sit on thrones at their wedding. They can build a house with mock Roman columns. They can be photographed, looking moody (him) and bored (her), at every party from Chigford to Burbank, and lavish extravagant birthday gifts on their children, but the Beckhams will only ever be Terry and June with a few bob.

In 2007, when Beckham left Madrid for LA Galaxy in a five-year deal worth £128 million all in, Timothy Leiweke, the president of AEG, the entertainment company that owns the club, said he would have 'a greater impact on soccer in America than any athlete has ever had on a sport globally'. Two years later, with Galaxy struggling, and sporting America untouched by the star in their midst, Beckham sought a move back to Europe, and found a new home in Milan. It was the act of a man who only ever thinks about himself.

This ludicrous pair are 'best friends' with Elton John, 'best friends' with Tom Cruise, 'best friends' with anybody who happens to be passing. In Madrid and Milan doors open because he is a well-known footballer. In LA, where football means grid-iron, and where she is merely the wife of who's-is?, talk of dining at the high table of showbiz was always misplaced.

Such longing for stardom is cyanide, as Giles understood. Not for the lady, whose role in life is to attend an endless round of fashion shows and parties, but for Beckham. Before he exchanged his soul for the foul dust of celebrity, he was a pretty good footballer.

9 George Best

Geoge Best may have been the finest footballer born in the British Isles. Although his career as a serious performer lasted only nine years, from 1963 to 1972, when he called time at the ripe old age of twenty-six to pursue the life of an international playboy, returning from time to time as a circus act, those who saw him in his glory days will never forget his mastery.

Claims for pre-eminence can be made on behalf of Tom Finney and Stanley Matthews, two wingers of an earlier age, though Best, like Finney, should not be restricted by so limited a description as 'winger'. He was a footballer, first and last, who could make and take goals with either foot, head the ball like a centre half, and tackle like a full back. That probably gave him the edge over Finney, although it is worth remembering that the Preston Plumber scored no fewer than thirty goals in his seventy-six appearances for England, usually from the left wing. He was still holding his own in his late thirties, when Best was struggling to hold his own with a barstool.

In a world context Best ranks pretty high. He doesn't belong in the elite group occupied by Pelé, Alfredo Di Stefano, Ferenc

Puskas and Diego Maradona. Nor is it right to bracket him with Johan Cruyff, Michel Platini and Zinedine Zidane, whose achievements are written in stone. Gerd Muller is the game's greatest goalscorer, and Marco van Basten is surely the finest centre forward there has ever been. So Best takes his place among the next group, which includes Eusebio, Luis Suarez and Gianni Rivera.

The young Best, nurtured by Matt Busby, was a bobby-dazzler. Football-lovers, not only Manchester United fans, still speak fondly of Best, Denis Law and Bobby Charlton, possibly to the irritation of younger generations, because they represented football at its purest. Charlton remains the best-loved of all English players. Law was a finisher supreme. Best, handsome, lithe, gifted beyond reason, offered a touch of fantasy. At his most imperious, between eighteen and twenty-five, it seemed there was nothing he could not do.

Those too young to have seen him in a red shirt will be more familiar with Best the 'character', which is one of the most tedious stories of our times, particularly when it is relived by bores in their cups. It is the reason he features in this list of infamy. Football, alone among games, offers casualties for the delight of a wider public, and Best did little to resist. The world-class performer became a world-class bore.

The most tiresome tale of all is the one about the hotel porter who produced champagne as Best was preparing for a night of rampant sex with one of the many Miss Worlds he squired, and wondered aloud 'where it had all gone wrong'. How everybody laughs at that one! Birds and booze for Besty. What a character!

It isn't funny. It is, in the truest sense, pathetic. With his looks and talent Best could pull any bird he wanted, and he did: usually the same one, over and over again. But whoever imagines compulsive fornication to be a life-affirming quality? It is a sign of weakness, just as surely as hopeless addiction to alcohol. A hero to so many when he had a ball at his feet, Best behaved like a fool off the field, dependent on the generosity of friends and the kindness of strangers. The Stanley Kowalski of Chorlton-cum-Hardy became the Blanche DuBois of SW3.

His talent was not for living, which, in his case, meant slow dying. It was for kicking a football. The leaving of Manchester, where he was bored to tears by the cheers, marked the beginning of a long decline he never tried hard enough to arrest. He could always trade on his fame, and the compound of celebrity and self-disgust, which was never far away, was lethal. Occasionally he vowed to mend his ways, but he never really meant it.

For a time he lived in America, where few people knew who he was. Then it was back to London, where he could be found propping up the bar at various pubs in Chelsea. Prevailed upon to speak at functions, or, on one infamous occasion, to appear on Terry Wogan's television show, he had to play the role of George Best, and although he could play it better than anybody else it devoured him. People wanted to think well of him because he had given so much pleasure to so many. It proved difficult.

We should remember the brilliant boy who arrived in Manchester from Belfast, and caught the mood of the Sixties. If Johnny Haynes was football's first major star of that decade, released from the prison of the maximum wage, Best became the game's first multi-media star, known simply as George, or Georgie.

That kind of fame, his allies have said, would have broken stronger men. Well, Pelé, a World Cup winner at seventeen, survived it. Perhaps we should be thankful for what Best gave us. We have to be. There was precious little to celebrate in the last three decades of a life that ended so desperately.

The cult of Best even ran to his funeral, which could have been mistaken for a state occasion. One might have thought the departed had been a great man, not an abnormally gifted footballer who had drowned his talent in a vat of booze. There is a difference.

10 Sid and Doris Bonkers

id and Doris have been friends of football for four decades. Created by Barry Fantoni for *Private Eye*, the batty couple are keen supporters of FC Neasden, managed by 'the ashen-faced supremo', Ron Knee, whose every thought is dutifully recorded by E. I. Addio, an old hack who files his copy from the car park.

In a strange development, some time in the autumn of 2008, Sid and Doris walked out of the *Eye*, rather like those characters in Woody Allen's film, *Purple Rose of Cairo*, who left the silver screen and assumed the dimensions of sentient beings. No longer were they to be found in Pricerite Road, home of the mighty Neasden. Instead they had shuffled along to the Emirates Stadium, the 60,000-seater home of Arsenal. It was difficult to recognise them at first in their handsome new surroundings but the moment they started giving Arsene Wenger the benefit of their advice ('Come off it, Wenger!'), there was no doubt.

Soon they had large sections of the crowd on their side. The Arsenal manager, previously regarded as untouchable, took some fearful stick for the folly of his selections, and the inadequacies of his players. For the rest of the season he had to put up with low-level grumbling that occasionally found more vocal expression. Spectators left the ground early, in a towering rage. Others stayed to boo the team off the field. The ones who were really vexed rang up radio phone-ins to tell the world that 'the boss' had 'lost the plot, big time'.

At the end of the season, Arsenal's fourth in a row without a trophy, some choleric shareholders confronted Wenger at the club's annual meeting. He, in turn, was sufficiently angry to consider an approach from Real Madrid, who were sniffing about like hungry boars. 'Every day,' he said, wistfully, 'you feel you have killed someone. What kind of world do we live in?' After sleeping on it he decided not to go to Spain, but perhaps he should have done, to teach those hobbledehoys a lesson.

It is worth reflecting on Wenger's question, for it reflects directly on the dolts who had the gall to criticise him. Looking back at the great managers English football has known he is fit to rank as a club-builder with Sir Matt Busby and Bill Shankly. Busby rebuilt Manchester United from the rubble of the Second World War. Shankly took over at Liverpool when they were in the Second Division. They were giants of the game, and so is Wenger. If the people who abused him cannot see what he has done for the club they claim to support there are no words strong enough to denounce their stupidity.

When Wenger went to Highbury in 1996 he joined a club synonymous with attritional football. Arsenal seemed to take pleasure from the fact that they had always been grim to watch, and would never mend their ways. Even their supporters, if they are honest, found it hard to stomach at times. Now they are everybody's second team. The football they have played under his supervision has been beautiful and, for much of the time, successful. Instead of boring everybody rigid, they have adorned the game.

Those who recall the Gunners' double-winning team of 1971, whose players were about as interesting to watch as a bunch of road-diggers, know just how much they owe to the man from Alsace. He arrived a year after George Graham, the builder of two champion sides, had been forced from office after he admitted taking £425,000 from the Norwegian agent, Rune Hauge, for the signings of John Jensen and Pal Lydersen.

Graham, who belonged to the 1971 team, was a champion as player and manager, a Highbury hero. But not many people were thrilled by the prospect of watching the sides he put out. He was strictly 'old Arsenal', the ones who kept the back door locked even when there was nothing in the house. Set against that context, Arsenal's liberation under Wenger has been the most remarkable football story of the past half-century. He has overturned a century of ivy-clad tradition. Yet their fans grumble!

There are cultural forces at work here. Hundreds of fans who sit in boxes at the Emirates (boxes built, by the way, on the back of funds generated by Wenger's success) did not know the old Highbury. In London, more than anywhere, football's financial resurgence since Year Zero, 1992, has attracted a new kind of supporter. After winning the championship in 1953 Arsenal went for sixteen seasons without winning anything, but nobody howled at the moon. Now the cry is: we want it all, and we want it now!

Some of these people are happy only when their team is winning week in, week out, and sport does not always grant one's most fervent wishes. They look at Manchester United and Chelsea, who have spent significantly more money, and wonder why the Gunners are not winning championships any more. Ah yes, it must be the manager, and his obsession with youth. Let's find another one.

This sense of entitlement, born out of impatience and ignorance, is not restricted to Arsenal. You can hear it at other grounds, where a poor run of matches will bring the manager a step closer to the block. It is more apparent at Arsenal because of the club's patrician traditions, doing the right thing and all that, and because of Wenger's magnificent work during a decade when he turned out one of the most watchable teams English football has ever seen. He spoiled them.

Begone, Sid and Doris Bonkers! Begone from the Emirates, and from all places where one-eyed ambition runs ahead of sense. Take your invective back to Neasden, where you can watch 'Baldy' Pevsner nod a few more past his own goalie. Tell Brigadier 'Buffy' Cohen, club chairman and local laundry magnate, what you think of him. As for the ingrates of N1, remember the precious gifts Wenger has showered into your laps. If your team never wins another match the man still deserves a dukedom.

11 Billy Bragg

Billy Bragg, songwriter and football fan, is happy to be known as a 'progressive patriot'. But, where football is concerned, what does patriotism mean?

In recent years England's passage to the final stages of major international tournaments has been accompanied by the appearance of the flags of St George. From cars and houses, shops and schools, pubs and even from public buildings, out they come, as though by some commissar's edict, when the national side is on the march. What does this flag-mania speak of? And to whom?

One thing is for sure. This is not England they are celebrating. It is not the land of Wordsworth and Gainsborough, Hardy and Constable, or of Chesterton, with his 'rolling English road'. It is not the rural idyll evoked by Vaughan Williams, or the view that Ray Davies spied from Waterloo Bridge. It is that other country, Ing-er-land, where the football fan can feel quite at home. After all, he more or less invented it.

In England, which has never been a land of flag-wavers, love of country is usually understated, absorbed slowly, and rooted in an unspoken affection for landscape, language and history.

It finds its clearest expression in folk memory of the village, with its church, green, pond and pub. That image may have become a cliché but clichés acquire their force for perfectly good reasons. We are not a people given to emotional excess, or we used not to be. Sometimes we give the impression that we can't be roused for anything, until we are forced to defend what we hold dearest. As an American journalist put it during the Second World War: 'The English can be relied upon to fall at every obstacle – except the last.'

So when the flags come out during a World Cup, the old-fashioned Englishman or woman tends to take a sceptical view. Why do we do this for football, and nothing else? Is this the only way an ancient country like ours can define itself? At one level, the answer may be yes. With the creation of a Scottish Parliament and a Welsh Assembly, the kingdom is less united than it was, and sport can offer some kind of emotional release, which in itself is no bad thing. Peoples like to come together. Everybody likes to see 'our side' do well.

There is a paradox here. Cricket, which has acquired a reputation for being a bit stuffy, because the public schools and universities have traditionally provided many of its best players, has become a far more effective symbol of a culturally diverse country than the more popular round-ball game. Through the immersion in it of players from Asian backgrounds, such as Nasser Hussain, the son of an Indian Muslim, who became a very English captain of England, it holds a more reliable mirror up to modern English society. Not a perfect one, but one that most of us recognise.

Nobody looks at the 'Barmy Army' on tour and fears for the old country. You may not like the noise they make, but they are not a malicious group. Nor are the people who go to the rugger. Twickenham Man may sometimes look a buffoon in his natural habitat, braying away lustily in his waxed barbour, but rugby folk are not one-eyed tribalists. However, when football covers itself in the flag it brings out all the baser elements, particularly when thousands of England fans gather in foreign cities where, oddly enough, the natives have customs of their own.

Bragg sees things differently. Appearing on Radio Four's *Today* programme before the European Championship of 2004, with the flags a-flutter, and the looser tongues predicting a glorious English triumph, he praised the emergence of a benign patriotism. The flags reclaimed English identity from the far right, and brought people together. The game, he went on, with rather more conviction than was wise, represented, along with the English language, our greatest gift to the world.

Bragg is not a silly man. In his book, *The Progressive Patriot*, which gives an account of growing up in Barking, he comes across as a decent stick. You could put him down as an old-fashioned working-class type, far removed from the perfumed bullshit of the pop world, with its adolescent urge to shock. However, by drawing his bow so wide on football's behalf, in the cause of a patriotism that is not always as benign as he might wish, he overplayed his hand.

By offering football as England's second most significant gift to the world, he conveniently overlooked, among many other things, parliamentary democracy, the rule of law, dozens of writers known throughout the world for using the language he so rightly admires, philosophers who prepared the ground for the Enlightenment, scores of scientists and engineers whose ideas have assisted mankind, and all manner of inventions from the seed drill to the worldwide web. England played a significant part in the Reformation, the Romantic Age and the Industrial Revolution. Twice the English (with a little help from our friends) saved Europe, first from Napoleon, then from Hitler. We did invent football, it is true, but then we gave the world every sport worth playing. The world has not withheld its gratitude.

It is characteristic of football's rampant egotism to take itself more seriously than is healthy, and the insidious way it has infiltrated the lower reaches of our national culture means that Bragg could utter something so silly, and not be put in the stocks of public opinion. But that is where he should be, for a day or two, to cool his heels. He's bright enough to see the error of his ways.

12 Ashley Cole

If you were looking for a prototype of the spoilt modern footballer, you might start at one of the top clubs, where, contrary to what we have been brought up to believe, money really does grow on trees. You might happen upon a gifted youngster, who became a first-team regular in his teens, and was soon promoted to international level.

You might not like the cut of his jib. You might think he was a bit too big for his boots, but you might excuse the flutter of feathers for his talent on the pitch, particularly if his efforts contributed to his team winning championships and FA Cups. Players don't have to get on. Supporters don't have to like them. Football teams have never been exercises in social harmony. They are constructed for one purpose, to win matches, though it is pleasing to win them with a smile.

You might not admire his decision to arrange a clandestine meeting with the manager and chief executive of another club who happened to have more money, and the lack of class to flaunt it. You might think that a player nurtured by a club from his schooldays should remain loyal to that club, unless there was something fundamentally wrong. In which case you might be amused when he was fined £100,000, reduced to £75,000 on appeal, for breaking Premier League rules. You might wonder why football people feel it necessary to meet in swanky restaurants when a more humble location would serve their interests better. A bench in Green Park, perhaps.

You might also wonder, not for the first time, what role agents play in all this malarkey. You might think that players do not always receive the best possible advice. But then you might think that a player who writes in his autobiography (or has written on his behalf) that he 'nearly drove off the road' when he heard his club were prepared to pay him only £55,000 a week to be incapable of acting sensibly upon any advice he might receive. You might recall Wilde's remark about knowing the price of everything and the value of nothing.

Knowing all this about the player, you might not be surprised that his behaviour did not improve, on or off the pitch, when he got the transfer across London he was angling for. It reached such a level of petulance that, having switched clubs, he abused a referee in the most explicit terms during a Premier League match, belittling Mike Riley in such a vile way that, by turning his back, he let the world know he had no respect for any kind of authority. The world was not surprised. As a consequence of his behaviour the Wembley crowd, upset by a blunder that led directly to the loss of a goal against Kazakhstan, decided to boo the offender. Not so much for the error, because all players make them. Rather, as a commentary on the player's conduct and general attitude over many years.

When he needed to reform his behaviour, it got worse. With

his wife, a pop singer, out of the country on a television jaunt he was found in a tired and emotional state one night outside a South Kensington bar. This time it was the police officers who felt the rough edge of his tongue, and he was taken to the cells, where payment of a statutory £80 fine earned his release. It did not release him from the judgment of the public, who convicted him for being drunk, disorderly – and a footballer.

The scorn intensified when it was reported that the player had been enjoying an 'intellectual discussion' with a young lady. For those familiar with the American popular songbook, it brought to mind the words Lorenz Hart put in the mouth of the bookish stripper in *Pal Joey*: 'I was reading Schopenhauer last night. And I think that Schopenhauer was right.' Eventually his intellect got the better of him. In February 2010, appalled by the number and manner of these 'discussiuons', on both sides of the Atlantic, his wife cast him out.

You might, weighing up all these things, think that Fabio Capello was speaking for everybody when he urged some of his players to grow up if they wanted to retain their places in the England team. You might go a bit further. You might wish that the manager had dropped the more poorly behaved of them, as a warning shot to the others. You might think the game has indulged far too long some rich young men whose manners leave much to be desired. Playing for your country is not a right. It is a privilege, or it used to be.

In short, anybody looking for a prototype of the spoilt modern footballer might start with Ashley Cole. If his brains were made of dynamite, you wouldn't trust him to blow his hat off.

13 Garry Cook

Clarity is all. That was the lesson George Orwell imparted in his great essay, 'Politics and the English Language', which should be absorbed not only by journalists, but also by politicians, and by all who hold responsibility for the instruction of young people. It would do Garry Cook no harm to read it, either.

Orwell knew that flim-flam merchants would cock a deaf 'un. Given the choice between cold water and hot air, the politician, the salesman, the impresario, will usually choose the latter. So will the sportsman. Orwell wrote another essay, a much-quoted one, about the nationalistic impulse of sport getting in the way of friendly rivalry – 'war minus the shooting'. Where games are concerned much of what passes for discourse is a form of deception.

The language of football was barren long before Cook came along. What, for instance, does 'different class' mean? Only that the person who uses such a tired phrase cannot be bothered to think. 'At the end of the day', 'there or thereabouts', 'down to the wire'. Meaningless, all of it, though humour can occasionally intrude. A manager on a losing run once attributed it to a lack of 'harmonium' in the dressing-room.

So far, so bad. Even so, nothing could prepare football fans for 'the project', an abstraction that entered the game's vocabulary in 2008. As so often we have Manchester City, jesters supreme, to thank. In their vainglorious quest to conquer world football by means of spending the riches first of a Thai of doubtful provenance, then an Arab billionaire, they recruited Cook to be their chief executive. Born in Birmingham, Cook had spent some years in America, working for Nike, the sportswear company, where he learned to say strange things with a straight face. Once installed at Eastlands he wasted no time in treating the football 'community' to the kind of guff you can acquire only in a world where people speak with no regard for meaning.

He had come to Manchester, he declared, to assist the City 'project'. Where football clubs had traditionally been about the players, with a little help from the people who coached them, people were now encouraged to think in terms of something altogether more noble. Nobody specified what the project was in words that could be understood. But, as Orwell wrote, the misuse of language is an attempt to give the appearance of solidity to pure wind.

For schoolchildren a project may conjure up images of following a geography teacher round a forest, looking at trees and flowers, or perhaps writing a history essay. Adults of a certain age may be reminded of Smersh agents in the Bond films, as 007 tried to foil baddies who wandered round underground bunkers in white coats, carrying clipboards and barking orders in foreign voices. What does not spring readily to mind is a football club.

After a while an outline of the project became visible. It had to with international 'brands': replica shirts and such like. City needed a few big names, players who would be known to television audiences in the Far East, where the markets were. Richard Dunne, said Cook, doesn't shift many shirts in Thailand. It was a fine way to reward the club's captain and player of the year who, for all his limitations as a defender, had given his all to the cause.

Cook's original benefactor was Thaksin Shinawatra, the former Prime Minister of Thailand, who had sought refuge in England after being ousted following a coup and being accused of corruption and abuse of power. Given this unhappy background one might have thought he was the sort of man the Premier League would disbar under their 'fit and proper person' rule. He was a rich man, though, which was good enough. It usually is.

Cheeky new bug Cook gave no mind to the allegations levelled at City's prosperous owner. Instead he treated newspaper reporters to a bizarre round-table interview, when he said that Shinawatra was a man with whom he would be happy to play golf. What are a few misdemeanours when there is that lovely 'project' to keep 'on track'? Anyway, Thailand is a long way away. It doesn't really count.

On and on Cook drove the City chariot, not Mark Hughes, the highly regarded manager the club had brought in from Blackburn Rovers. In no time he established a reputation as one of the game's choicest buffoons, no mean feat for one so wet behind the ears. It was a reputation he was to confirm in champion style when he flew to Milan to sign Kaka, the Brazilian striker, for a cool £100 million. Hughes had already been sidelined in the swoop for another Brazilian striker, Robinho. Now the manager was obliged to watch open-mouthed as the club's chief executive, employing his years of experience in the world of contracts and image rights, blundered into an Italian trap.

Despite the banging of drums, peal of trumpets, and careful manipulation of the media, the project manager didn't even meet Kaka. Instead he was given the chance to explain the Big P to the player's representatives, who politely declined the offer on behalf of their absent friend. Rebuffed, Cook flew home to Manchester, accusing Milan, seven times the champions of Europe, of lacking professionalism. They didn't even serve biscuits as we were kept waiting, he moaned. Anyway, he said, Kaka wouldn't have got into the City first team. Stephen Ireland would have kept him out. Who knows? One day the provincial clod-hoppers of Milan might measure up to the lofty standards for which Manchester City are so well known.

It was a terrific hoot while it lasted, though the Arabs whose limitless funds underwrite the City project were less than pleased with their chief executive's cavalier conduct. Kaka later signed for Real Madrid, another of those clubs who don't go in for fig rolls and jaffa cakes. When you've won the European Cup nine times you can please yourselves. Hughes, meanwhile, was sacked for not living up to expectations, and replaced by Roberto Mancini.

Undeterred, Cook carried on briefing reporters about the plans he was drawing up, night and day, for global domination, as he told a meeting of City supporters in a Manhattan pub called, appropriately, The Mad Hatter Saloon. After that, no doubt, he will arrange a trip to the moon on gossamer wings. Particularly if there's a golf course up there.

14 Hunter Davies

Writing about football, as opposed to football writing, has been a mixed bag. The world's most popular sport has inspired few outstanding books. Perhaps the finest one by an English author remains Arthur Hopcraft's *The Football Man*, a kaleidoscopic view of the national game written in 1968, when England were world champions. Four decades later it can be read as the map of a foreign land.

Leo McKinstry has written two fine books, a biography of Sir Alf Ramsey and a portrait of the Charltons called, simply, *Jack and Bobby*. Neither Charlton spoke to the author but the generous testimony of team-mates and opponents enabled McKinstry to shape a handsome evocation of the recent past, and remind readers what glorious careers the brothers enjoyed.

In recent years another, confessional kind of book has blossomed. Nick Hornby kicked it off in 1992 with *Fever Pitch* and even if one thinks his tale of adolescence was overrated there can be no denying that he touched a nerve. Hornby gets a couple of marks at least for telling a story that found echoes in so many lives.

Others have been less successful. One recalls with something less than affection *All Played Out* by Pete Davies. The author trotted off to the 1990 World Cup hoping to find a 'narrative' that matched the one he had already sketched in his mind: to wit, England, as a land, was 'all played out'. Here was football as metaphor. Instead England reached the semi-finals, where they lost on penalties to the Germans, and Davies was left feeling patriotic and broken-hearted.

The man who began this confessional writing, from a fan's perspective, was Hunter Davies. He made his name as a journalist in the Sixties, cashed in with a biography of the Beatles, and, in 1972, he wrote *The Glory Game* about a season in the life of Tottenham Hotspur. It was a decent read. Unfortunately it had the consequence of making Davies believe that, because he was a supporter, more specifically a Spurs fan, he had been granted a unique insight into the world of football.

Since then he has written at length about the game, and got gradually worse. His breathless, sentimental pieces are littered with unremarkable first-person observations, and his jokes wouldn't pass muster in a sixth-form gang show. 'When I first heard of catenaccio,' he has written, 'I really did think it was some sort of Italian frothy coffee.' In that case, Hunter lad, you were on your own.

In recent years his guff about 'Wayne' and 'Paul', with whom he worked as a helpful, energetic ghost, has been dismal, although, to be fair, he caught the tone of Gascoigne's voice in that sad man's autobiography. It just wasn't worth listening to. In Rooney's case a £5 million five-book deal was knocked down to two after the first volume of his life's story (at the age of twenty-one) failed to catch fire. It's hard to blame Davies for that. You just wonder why he feels the need to do it when he could be bounding across the Cumbrian fells.

Working with Rooney and Gascoigne must be a bit of a comedown after knowing the Fab Four. But what Davies really knows about is himself. One of his books is called *Football, the Beatles and Me*, and he has always considered the third element at least as important as the first two. Sometimes you get the impression that he was in the studio, toasting crumpets with George Martin, adjusting the level as 'the boys' made *Revolver*.

Yet, unwittingly, Davies has had more influence than many better writers. The 'fan's view', which originally found expression in the 1970s satirical magazine *Foul*, became more prominent in the 1980s with the rise of the fanzines, which were exactly what they appeared to be: magazines written in a breezy style by and for fans. Some of the copy was funny. Some of it was not. It was all a bit of a wheeze.

To the extent that supporters were entitled to have a say about their club, the fanzines worked. Local papers can tell readers only so much, and club programmes are designed to reveal nothing at all. In time, though, the fans acquired a voice that was neither funny nor warm. You can read that voice today in the blogs on websites established by supporters, and on the websites of national newspapers. It has even infiltrated mainstream football reporting.

Admirers of the blog call it 'citizens' journalism', and there is clearly a place for it. Many political stories have come directly from the blogosphere, with occasionally devastating consequences at Westminster. In football's case it can be like playing with fire. Many comments left by fans are deeply offensive to the players and supporters of other clubs, and sometimes their own. Some posts are actionable.

Obviously Davies is not responsible for the cruelty and puerility of the blogs posted by those odd people who stay up half the night trawling through the internet, hoping to be offended. But, in his modest way, he helped to start something that is unhealthy: the football fan's obsession with himself, and his unshakable belief that the club he follows is the centre of the universe. Now that the portals are open, all sorts of half-wits have marched in.

You could argue that many fans have always been 'intellectually challenged'. That doesn't let Davies off the hook. He has never written well enough to earn the benefit of the doubt.

15 Didier Drogba

It isn't difficult to make enemies when you are a highly paid footballer. In a tribal world of strong attachments and entrenched views being good can mark a man out for the abuse of the multitudes. Many players get it in the neck. But it is doubtful that any of them is so widely reviled as Didier Drogba.

A gifted, athletic striker, who has contributed many fine goals to Chelsea's success since his arrival from Marseille in 2004, the man from the Côte d'Ivoire has earned the contempt of all who wish to see football played the right way. 'The right way' is not some Corinthian ideal. It doesn't mean applauding opponents when they have scored, or offering three cheers at the end. It means acknowledging that the game is bigger than all those who play it, that there are standards players transgress at their peril. It is a test Drogba has flunked miserably.

When he is not scoring goals, Drogba is diving. When he is not diving, he is sulking. When he is not diving or sulking, he is pouting like an Old Compton Street tart. When he is not diving, sulking or pouting, he is dropping public hints about rejoining the manager who signed him, Jose Mourinho. It is unusual for fans of any club to turn against their own but

Chelsea's do not care much for the centre forward who has helped to win two Premier League titles, two FA Cups and two League Cups. His petulance, on display every time he fails to get his own way, damns him as a show-pony.

He has the rosettes to prove it. Chelsea would almost certainly have won the Champions League in 2008 if Drogba had managed to behave like an adult. Instead he was sent off two minutes from the end of extra time after slapping Nemanja Vidic, the Manchester United defender. Drogba, who would have taken one of Chelsea's penalties in the shoot-out, flounced off with a flap of his tail. John Terry, obliged to fill the breach, struck the post with his kick, and United were champions of Europe. That unnecessary dismissal really was one for the team.

Sent off in a Champions League match in Barcelona three years previously, Drogba has form when it comes to letting his team-mates down. It's not just Chelsea he has failed. Unless others see the world the way it appears to his eyes he withholds his consent. In English football, which, for all its faults, engenders a spirit of comradeship, there is no greater offence.

When Mourinho left Chelsea in 2007 Drogba wanted to follow his benefactor out of Stamford Bridge, saying 'something is broken'. It was not a comment designed to maintain harmony. Two years later, in the weeks before Luiz Felipe Scolari was sacked, Drogba could barely lift a leg. His performance in a match at Old Trafford was pitiful. Yet no sooner had Guus Hiddink been appointed than the show-pony was galloping around like a frisky colt. Scolari, it was put about, had 'lost' the dressing-room. It's not hard to do, even for World Cup winners, when players get a strop on. Good professionals, on the other hand, pull their boots on and play.

Whatever else he will be remembered for at Chelsea, Drogba will never be allowed to forget two incidents, four years apart, that shone an unflattering spotlight on his character. In 2005, pressed by a television interviewer to answer accusations that he threw himself to the ground too often, he replied: 'Sometimes I dive, sometimes I stand.' He was advised to withdraw the comment but his retraction lacked conviction. In a game cursed by divers, Drogba may well be the most enthusiastic of the lot. He probably dived out of the womb, and snapped at the midwife.

In May 2009 came the most petulant act of all. Substituted during the second half of a Champions League semi-final against Barcelona at Stamford Bridge, Drogba retired to the bench. After Barcelona snatched an equaliser in injury time, to reach the final on away goals, he directed his fury at the Norwegian referee, Tom Henning Ovrebo, in a way that would have embarrassed a toddler. Addressing the television cameras he then uttered abuse of the kind that toddlers do not use, along the lines that the official had been 'a disgrace'. And who better to tell him?

Naturally, with another suspension looming (he eventually received a six-match ban), another diplomatic apology was forthcoming. There was even support from the dressing-room. In the amoral world of professional football, there always is. Press officers and agents are always on hand to tell players who have spoken hastily to temper their views, and look suitably ashamed. But when Drogba let the world know his behaviour was unworthy of his rank, few were prepared to take his side. The evidence against him was so overwhelming that he could have said four fours were sixteen and nobody would have believed him.

Nobody can deny that this excitable chap is a talented footballer. His record proves as much. But he is a very bad hat indeed. A disgrace, you might say.

16 Martin Edwards

The formation of the Premier League in 1992 was football's equivalent of the 1832 Reform Act. There was football before the Premier League, and there was football afterwards, but things were not the same. The Premier League, boosted by the riches of Sky Television, has swept away the old order. A younger generation of football fans has grown up knowing nothing of the Four Divisions, and the (largely) fraternal spirit of the old days.

From a historical point of view the comparison is not exact. The Reform Act opened a door that led eventually to universal suffrage, which must be a good thing unless one holds Voltaire's view that it is better to be ruled by a lion than a thousand rats. The Premier League is not about democracy at all. It is about power: the power of the few. Whether that has brought wider benefits to English football is a matter for conjecture. It certainly hasn't done much for the welfare of the national side, which was one of the aims stated quite openly when the elite division was established.

There were many hands in events leading up to the big bang. In 1981 the Football Association, guardians of the game since

1863, relaxed the prohibition, drawn up in their 1900 handbook, that 'no director shall be entitled to receive any remuneration in respect of his office'. So long as they worked full-time at their club, directors could now be paid.

Two years later, the Football League did away with gate-sharing, a change which benefited the bigger clubs. It was also the year that Tottenham Hotspur floated shares on the Stock Exchange. There was no need any longer for Chinese whispers. The bigger clubs were quite brazen about forming a Premier League, which duly came about in 1992.

David Dein, vice-chairman of Arsenal, and a key member of the Football League management committee, is generally credited with playing a significant part in its creation. But the most revealing comment, that stripped the bride bare, so to speak, came from Martin Edwards, then the chairman, later the chief executive of Manchester United. 'The smaller clubs', he said, with chilling matter-of-factness, 'are bleeding the game dry. For the sake of the game, they should be put to sleep.'

Of course it all depends on what you mean by a small club. Compared with Manchester United most clubs look small, in terms of popular appeal; even Arsenal. What Edwards meant was that too many clubs in the lower divisions were draining the game of money. He and his chums wanted more of it, to dispose of as they saw fit, and in Rupert Murdoch they found the right man at the right time.

For a man who inherited the chairman's role at Old Trafford in 1980 because he was his father's son, Edwards has done very well for himself. Louis Edwards made his fortune by selling dodgy meat. Martin has known some dodgy times, too. In 2002 he was reported to Greater Manchester Police after following a lady to the toilet at the Mottram Hall Hotel, near Prestbury, and spying on her. Other witnesses to similar incidents at Old Trafford emerged to allege that Edwards had previous in this respect. Exposed by this episode, Edwards stood down as chairman. The following year he sold his remaining shares in United, taking his profit over the year to more than £100 million, and became the club's honorary life president.

Edwards should not be hanged for his private affairs, though, whatever the truth may be, the private domain touches on the public if you are the figurehead of a club like Manchester United. Reports of him using a prostitute on club business during a trip to Switzerland in 2002 was not therefore best for the career of a man paid handsomely to represent England's biggest club. Edwards was tolerated by the majority of United's fans, because he brought Alex Ferguson to Old Trafford in 1986, and supported the manager through some difficult early days. But he never enjoyed their affection.

In 1984 he was ready to hand the club over to Robert Maxwell, whose probity is a matter of public record. Five years later he opened the club's books to the mysterious Michael Knighton, who could have bought the club for £10 million if he had found somebody to lend him the money. Old Trafford gathered its breath, and Knighton went off after a year or two to turn another United, Carlisle, into world-beaters.

When Murdoch's BSkyB came knocking in 1998 the money was all there, in crisp notes, but the Monopolies Commission intervened to rule out the takeover, which would have yielded Edwards £98 million. He sold the last of his equity in 2000, and made more than £100 million over the years from his shareholding, so the rugby-playing butcher's son has done pretty well out of United, though he might argue that, as the man who stood by Ferguson at a time of uncertainty, the club has also done pretty well out of him. He might also say that, no matter what happened on his watch, he did less damage than the Glazer clan, whose refinancing of the club left United £716 million in debt.

The Reform Act cleaned up all those rotten boroughs. Football's rotten boroughs have not been banished by Murdoch's billions. They have simply bought a different kind of serfdom. At the end of the 2007/8 season the Premier League clubs were in debt to the tune of £3.1 billion.

Remember those words: 'The smaller clubs are bleeding the game dry. For the sake of the game, they should be put to sleep.' When you read them, you can almost hear the sound of jackboots.

17 Sven-Goran Eriksson

Sven-Goran Eriksson isn't a bad chap. According to Ulrika Jonsson, one of the ladies who managed to sneak into his domestic compound when Nancy Dell'Olio was looking the other way, he used to stack the washer each night, and which woman wouldn't want a man like that? 'Have you loaded the pots, dear?' Cocoa, slippers, and so to bed, Mr Pepys.

No, Eriksson wasn't a bad chap. The problem is, he wasn't terribly good. Brought in as England's first foreign manager in January 2001, after a successful club career with Gothenburg, Benfica and Lazio, the Swede proved a disappointing leader. Given that no England manager can possibly satisfy the demands of voracious media and the footballing public, he still fell shorter of the desired mark than he should have done.

His record at international tournaments was modest, though he did at least take England to the finals on three occasions. In the 2002 World Cup England went out to Brazil in the quarter-final, despite taking the lead through Michael Owen and having the undeniable advantage of playing with eleven men against Brazil's ten after Ronaldinho, the scorer of what turned out to be the winner, had been sent off.

Two years later England lost on penalties to Portugal, the host nation, in the quarter-final of the European Championship. Then, in 2006, they lost a World Cup quarter-final in the same manner to the same opponents after Wayne Rooney had been dismissed. After that Eriksson took his leave, though he continued to be paid for another year by the Football Association.

His major weakness was an inability to bind David Beckham within the fabric of a team game. Beckham could do no wrong by Eriksson, with the inevitable consequence that other players, who contributed as much, or more, felt resentment at their captain's preferential treatment.

Beckham should not have been captain at all. The World Cup defeat by Brazil was due in part to Beckham's decision to pull out of a tackle in the dying seconds of the first half. Granted a chance to maintain the attack, Ronaldinho made a chance for Rivaldo, who equalised. In Portugal two years later it was Beckham who hoofed a penalty over the crossbar in the shoot-out. By 2006 he was a shadow of the player who had once turned heads, yet he retained the manager's loyalty.

When players were brought into the team Eriksson still stood behind Beckham, whose powers had begun to wane when he left Old Trafford for Real Madrid in 2003. Even when Shaun Wright-Phillips, who plays in the same right-sided position as Beckham, was given a rare chance, he had to play out of position as Eriksson could not bring himself to drop his favourite.

If Beckham was indulged in a manner that no player should ever be, another midfield player was denied the chance to show off his skills to best effect. Paul Scholes, the most gifted English footballer of his generation, should have been the key man in Eriksson's team. Instead he was shunted on to the left side of the midfield 'diamond', so that Frank Lampard and Steve Gerrard could have opportunities galore to prove they cannot play together.

Lampard and Gerrard are fine players, even if they tend to leave their club form behind when they pull on an England shirt. But Scholes could and should have been a world-beater. Sidelined by Eriksson, he retired from international football in 2004, citing 'family reasons'. He had a good England career. With a bit more sensitivity from the man who picked the team it could have been a great one.

The 5–1 thumping of Germany in September 2001 bought Eriksson a lot of goodwill early in his tenancy. But England never built on the promise of that night. Too often they were timid. Even when Brazil were a man down, and ready to be attacked at will, England could not raise a gallop. Eriksson merely sat there, looking uninvolved.

His lack of apparent involvement counted against him in the saloon bar of public debate (which, admittedly, is not always edifying). But he became very involved indeed when club sides showed an interest.

Eriksson was spotted twice conducting talks with representatives of Chelsea. On the first occasion, in July 2003, it was the big cheese himself, Roman Abramovich. In March 2004 it was Peter Kenyon, the club's chief executive, that he met. He said they were social meetings. But it was foolish behaviour. An England manager, particularly a foreign hireling, should not be seen having social meetings with such people. The FA, eager to keep him on a tighter leash, increased his salary to £4 million year.

Eriksson wasn't worth the money. He did a half-decent job when, with a bit more gumption, and a bit less favouritism, he could have turned England into European champions. He outstayed his welcome – by about five years.

In 2008, after a fair-to-middling year at Manchester City, he found a new home, with the Mexican national team, but that too proved to be a year-long engagement. To everybody's surprise the millionaire globe-trotter returned to English football in July 2009, as the man in charge of Notts County, in the old Fourth Division. It couldn't last, and it didn't. Within six months, after a change of owners, he was on the road again.

18 'The Fans'

Once in a while it is a good idea to send an outsider to events usually covered by specialists. A fresh pair of eyes may find a perspective that others take for granted, or fail to see at all. When the BBC dispatched Jonathan Agnew to watch an afternoon of sport in Leicester in 1997 it turned out to be more than a good idea. It was a revelation.

Agnew, the BBC's cricket correspondent, had been a professional cricketer for Leicestershire and England, so he knew the territory. Yet what he saw that day shocked him, and his response made for an unforgettable radio report. His task was simple: to watch Leicester Tigers take on Bath, and then walk along Welford Road to see Leicester City play Manchester United.

At the rugby both sets of fans mingled happily in the pubs beforehand, and there were no police officers inside the ground, though there were a few stewards, for form's sake. The mood was jolly, and the afternoon passed off peacefully. Down the road Agnew saw hundreds of spectators baiting each other before, during and after the game. Had they not been strictly segregated, a physical separation enforced by dozens of police officers and stewards, there would have been a riot.

Although his observations would not have surprised many
people who follow the round-ball game, Agnew was clearly
puzzled. He left several questions unasked, but they remained
hanging in the air. Why were those who followed the two
sports so different? Why can a rugby chap enjoy a gallon of
ale and entertain his neighbour while a football fan wants to
tear the other's head off when he is sober? They are only games.

Later that year a more forensic witness was in the Olympic
Stadium, Rome, to watch England play Italy in a World Cup
qualifying match. Anthony Daniels, a prison doctor until his
retirement, has forged a second career as a writer. Wearing his
journalistic hat he has become one of England's most clear-
eyed social commentators. If you see society at its worst, as he
did, your writing is supported by a depth of personal experience.
It helps that Daniels, a man of wide and deep learning, who
has spent much of his life working in the poorest parts of the
world, writes with the clarity of a born witness. Despite his
first-hand knowledge of poverty, he has often said, the most
deprived form of human life he has observed is in inner-city
England.

That night in Rome, he wrote, thousands of England fans
shouted obscenities 'in unison for hours on end'. Unlike Agnew,
he was not surprised by the 'deeply unattractive' people he
found himself among, except in two ways. 'The first was that
many among them were well-educated, and the second was
that, when the carabinieri charged, they immediately began to
feel self-pity and injured outrage. It was as if their inalienable
right to behave like scum had been unfairly challenged.'

Note well that last sentence. Anybody who has watched football in the past four decades will recognise its veracity, though we are not supposed to mention such things. Within the game people talk about 'passion' as though it belonged exclusively to football. 'Commitment' and other nebulous terms are used to exculpate behaviour that would not be tolerated in any other sport, or any other part of public life.

If it is a criminal offence to use insulting, threatening and abusive language then thousands of folk who attend football grounds on Saturday afternoons should appear in court on Monday morning. They don't because everybody, from the police down, has come to accept Saturday-afternoon bigotry as an acceptable price to pay. Why else are grounds segregated? Why are players instructed, on pain of dismissal, not to 'incite' crowds? (How, one may ask, do you incite people so eager to be incited?) And why do reporters sentimentalise those crowds, with talk of 'anthems' and 'choirs'?

The people who cause trouble, we are told, represent only a 'minority'. Then it must be a pretty large minority because, down the years, English yobs have rampaged through every corner of Europe, shattering the peace of countless cities, happy to blame others for every shard of broken glass. It is a wonder the national side is allowed to play anywhere.

This has nothing to do with drink. The Irish, who can be thirsty, follow their team all over the world, and have always settled their bar bills on departure, with requests from the hosts to come again. In rugby, as Agnew saw, supporters sup long into the night without fear of a word out of place. Any hint of nastiness is nipped in the bud by the spectators themselves. There is no need for police activity. The spectators police themselves.

Nor has it to do with social class. Rugby league, the one truly working-class sport in England, is watched by the best-behaved fans. Football people do not like to be told that because it reminds them of the pig-sty they have made, a sty in which they are happy to roll. 'Passion' indeed! That most overrated of human qualities makes a cosy bolt-hole for scoundrels.

Something else has happened in recent years. Daniels saw it on that grisly night in Rome, where he found in the behaviour of well-heeled England supporters 'a symptom of a deep and rapidly advancing cultural phenomenon: the proletarianisation of British life'. Ding dong! We may not lead the world at football but we are unbeatable champions when it comes to inverted snobbery.

This is Daniels on the people he saw in Rome, who may be found each week at any football ground in England: 'They think of their savagery as a kind of democratic virtue, a proof that they do not hold themselves above the common man. Hence their surprise, outrage and disbelief when they are treated by foreigners as the most degraded specimens of humanity they have ever encountered.'

Black ball into middle pocket.

19 Paul Gascoigne

It is permissible for sportsmen to weep in public, if they are winners. The shedding of tears may, in the right context, deepen the moment of triumph. In defeat it tends to reveal weakness of character. When Paul Gascoigne wept during the World Cup semi-final against Germany in June 1990, knowing that the booking he had just picked up meant he would not play in the final if England got there, it provided a more illuminating self-portrait than any number of outstanding performances could.

Gascoigne was a gifted player, who never became the great one he might have been. He has only himself to blame for that. His grotesque tackle on Gary Charles in the 1991 FA Cup final robbed him of the chance to justify the promise he had hinted at in his early performances for Newcastle, Tottenham and England. It had a significant effect on Charles's career, too. Like the man who fouled him, the Nottingham Forest defender ended up drunk.

Up to a point Gascoigne was a victim. He could have received better advice from agents and friends, and certainly needed firmer handling by his managers, one of whom, Bobby Robson,

called him 'daft as a brush'. It raised a laugh but Gascoigne did not need cheap laughter. There was too much of that, and over the years it turned sour. This impressionable, easily led man required somebody to say 'No'. Until Glenn Hoddle dropped him from the England team he never found one.

He could have kept better company, in Newcastle and London. Going out on the lash with media pals was no way for an international footballer to behave. Ultimately, though, he was the victim of his own weakness. Whatever his psychological problems, it is hard to have much sympathy for a man who has worked his way through the millions Gascoigne earned.

The tears he shed that night in Turin revealed the emotional instability of a man-child who never really grew up. Gascoigne could never understand how his conduct might offend others, even when he shouted obscenities into a microphone. However, once it was explained to him that he had erred he showed contrition. So he oscillated between extremes of behaviour, fuelled by alcohol, when what he really needed was the equilibrium that enables most people to live like adults. He was both childlike and childish.

It could be said the age looked more kindly upon his indiscretions than previous generations would have done. Gascoigne became football's performing flea in the decade that Princess Diana, the outstanding symbol of emotional grandstanding, was granted international superstar status. After her sad death in August 1997, which gave rise to such stomach-turning obsequies, modish commentators talked about 'emotional literacy'. For many English people, appalled by the scenes of public mourning, it was a language they had no intention of learning.

Compassion, genuine concern for others, ennobles people. Abstract grief for strangers diminishes them, and this grief, whipped up by newspapers and television, has become an ignoble feature of English life. Witness the ghastly, media-managed funerals of Jade Goody, who achieved a spurious kind of notoriety on the back of her Olympian ignorance, and Michael Jackson, the boy who never grew up. There is quite a lot of daylight between Gascoigne's decline and the choreographed stupidity of Goody, but the pair share a connection. Like so many whose lives lack discipline, they were unable to control their feelings.

Gascoigne, who admitted beating his wife, could not manage his life as a young man in Newcastle, in his maturity at Tottenham, or in his retirement. As for his three years in Rome, when he played for Lazio, it was not the wisest decision to spend so much time in the company of his drinking pals from Newcastle. Wherever he went Gascoigne sought to replicate the domestic circumstances of his youth, another indication of his unwillingness to grow up. The Tiber, alas, is nothing like the Tyne. The Piazza Navona is a long way from the Bigg Market.

He was certainly no ambassador. In 1996 there was the infamous dentist's chair routine, where he poured grog down his throat to hoots of laughter from other members of the England team. Two years later, brought low by a loss of form that persuaded Hoddle to leave him out of the World Cup squad, Gascoigne went berserk, smashing up the manager's hotel room. It was the final act of an international career that had carried the seed of something truly impressive. In the 1990 World Cup it seemed that England had found an attacking midfield player of uncommon talent. Nobody ever saw the best of that young man.

In the years since that desperate farewell Gascoigne has cut an increasingly forlorn figure. He drifted out of football, going down the leagues a step at a time, and drifted into the Priory. Then he was off to a clinic for alcohol dependency in Arizona. All the while people tried to help him. He was employed as a pundit by ITV for the World Cup in 2002, but was so incoherent that he had to be withdrawn. In 2005 Kettering Town appointed him manager. He lasted all of thirty-nine days. The bottle got in the way.

Eventually, in 2008, he was sectioned under the Mental Health Act for his own good. He promised to reform, and claimed at one stage that he was writing poetry. But there are always bars to prop up, and people who are happy to pick up the tab. This tale was never going to have a happy ending, so obvious were the flaws in Gascoigne's character. Here is a man who had almost everything, and threw it all away. Shed tears if you want. It won't do much good.

20 'Geordie Blubber'

The North East occupies a special place in the life of the nation. The Roman form of Christianity was confirmed at the Synod of Whitby in 664. St Cuthbert of Lindisfarne eased the process of conversion. The Venerable Bede, who wrote the *Ecclesiastical History of the English People*, is acknowledged throughout Christendom as one of the great scholars.

Durham Cathedral, a jewel of Norman architecture, which houses the shrine to St Cuthbert, is one of the great buildings of Europe. It formed the centrepiece of one of Kenneth Clark's television programmes in his celebrated study of *Civilisation*. Dull of soul is the person who fails to feel a sense of awe in the presence of such majesty.

From a geographical point of view it is also distinguished. The Northumberland coastline is regarded, not just by locals, as the finest in the kingdom. Hadrian's Wall, designed to keep out the troublesome Picts, is superb walking country. Here is a place of history and grandeur. Castles galore. Friendly folk. It must be a good place to live.

In recent years too many fans of Newcastle United have given outsiders a different impression. By demonstrating

emotional incontinence whenever their side has lost a match, which has happened quite a lot, they have let themselves down. The sight of supporters having a jolly good blub, which never fails to attract the attention of television producers looking for post-match 'colour', has ensured that 'Geordie Blubber' has become a well-known and, if truth be known, much-mocked character.

Mr Blubber belongs, we are told, to an ahistorical entity known as the 'Geordie Nation', though it is not a province that St Cuthbert would have recognised. We have Sir John Hall, the businessman and former Newcastle chairman, to thank for amplifying that horrid description, and more supporters have taken up the notion as geographical fact than is helpful. Now the phrase is trotted out without discrimination as though one could find it on the map, and, sadly for the majority of Novocastrians, who live blameless lives, it has become familiar to football followers as the home of our tear-stained friends in the north.

The miners and steelworkers who watched Newcastle win three FA Cups in five seasons in the Fifties did not weep whenever the ball went in their goal. The sorry tale began to unfold in 1992 when Kevin Keegan, a much-decorated former player, was persuaded to return to St James' Park as manager. The crowds had dropped to 14,000, and relegation to the Third Division was a possibility. Keegan kept them up, took them into the Premier League, and, for the next four seasons, turned out some highly watchable teams. In 1996 they should have won the title.

It was not Keegan's fault that he was proclaimed as 'the Messiah'. Language has always been a devalued currency in football. But the way in which Newcastle's supporters have opted to bankrupt themselves, year after year, has been alarming. Since Keegan's departure in 1997 each of his successors has been wafted into town on a carpet of lofty claims and pie-in-the-sky hopes. Ruud Gullit, Kenny Dalglish, Graeme Souness and Sir Bobby Robson were all hired and fired before Keegan returned to placate the cheering mob. Those men are some of the biggest names in the game, but it made little difference. When they reached the FA Cup Final in 1998, and again the following May, Newcastle surrendered to Arsenal and Manchester United in the most abject manner.

Yet each new manager is anointed as king of the Tyne. When Alan Shearer, a wonderful centre forward in the Newcastle cause, took the reins in March 2009 thousands appeared outside St James' to put a crown on his head. It didn't do them much good, as those outside the area could have told them it wouldn't. Some did tell them, but they were ignored. A Geordie was coming home, and God was in his Heaven. Two months later Newcastle were relegated ignominiously, after winning one of Shearer's eight games in charge. The club has now gone fifty-five years without winning a domestic trophy.

There is a lot of talk, much of it sentimental, about Newcastle letting down their supporters. But some of those supporters are part of the problem, for their expectations are impossible to fulfil. After Robson was sacked, having taken the club to a fifth place that was considered unacceptable for such a 'big' club, one of those puddled fans who turn up for the ritual coronations told television viewers that the Newcastle job was 'one of the biggest three in Europe'.

When some observers say those fans deserve 'better', it is wise to remember that tosh and say: no, not all of them do. Thousands, dazzled by silly talk of a Geordie Nation, will remain part of the problem until they revise their expectations. Newcastle is not a big club, if size is determined by achievement. It is a club with a proud history loved by thousands of people.

Geordie Blubber deserves some sympathy. Newcastle have wasted millions on poor players, and the men who have run the club have taken out a few bob more in salaries and perks. After Sir John Hall came Freddy Shepherd, and after him came Mike Ashley, who thought that tipping up to games in one of the replica shirts he flogs at Lillywhite's was a ripping wheeze. He also appointed the London-based Dennis Wise as director of football. Well played, gentlemen. You have all played a part in the farce.

Yet sympathy is a finite quality where Newcastle are concerned, and Geordie Blubber has earned his place in this inglorious parade. He's not difficult to spot, as he wears a black and white shirt in all seasons. When it is cold he likes to take it off. At all times he carries a freshly peeled onion.

21 'The Golden Generation'

On a balmy Munich evening in September 2001 a remarkable thing happened. England beat Germany. They did not just beat them, they pulverised them, scoring five goals to Germany's one. All five came from the boots of Liverpool players. Michael Owen bagged a hat-trick, and there was a goal apiece for Steven Gerrard and, to general amazement, Emile Heskey, who usually wears a blindfold in the penalty area.

With a World Cup to be staged in Japan and South Korea the following summer the English contingent in the Olympic Stadium scoured the night sky for auguries, like so many Herods with laptops. The players were anointed as the 'golden generation' and would, in time, make all England proud; maybe even win the World Cup. Not immediately, but some day, an Englishman would hold the cup aloft, just as Bobby Moore had accepted the old Jules Rimet Trophy from the Queen on that blissful day in 1966.

England did not win the World Cup the following summer. They went out to the ten men of Brazil in the quarter-finals after taking the lead. How did the vanquished Germans do? They reached the final, where, without the suspended Michael

Ballack, whose goal had won the semi-final, they lost to Brazil. Oliver Kahn, who had been in outstanding form between the posts, conceded a soft goal to Ronaldo, who promptly added a second. Germany's appearance in their seventh final, with a side considered to be modest, underlined one of football's greatest truths: they make the most of what they have got. The English do not.

Those who looked for a touch of humility within the English camp were crying for the moon. Without the camp, too. Some deluded fans still wear t-shirts that proclaim the 5–1 victory, when heads were well and truly turned. Gary Lineker, a fine goal-poacher in his day, used his newspaper column in the run-up to the 2006 World Cup to declare that England boasted no fewer than six 'world-class' players, which came as a bit of a surprise to those who thought that 'world-class' meant something more than domestic stardom.

When England won the World Cup they had five players who could be considered absolute top-notchers: Moore, Bobby Charlton, Gordon Banks and Ray Wilson belonged to that champion team. Jimmy Greaves, the greatest goalscorer England has ever produced, did not. He lost his place during the tournament and watched the final from the substitutes' bench. So Lineker's claim had to be taken with a barrel of salt.

Facts can be used to make all sorts of cases but they are fairly clear when it comes to the deeds of the men who played in Munich. England went no further in the 2006 World Cup than they did four years before, losing on penalties to Portugal, who had also knocked them out of the European Championship (on penalties) in 2004. Never mind, people said, all roads led to the lakes and mountains of Austria and Switzerland, where the European Championship of 2008 would be taking place. The roads did indeed lead there but England could not pluck sprigs of edelweiss for their Alpine hats. Beaten home and away by Croatia, who reminded the Wembley crowd that football is essentially about possession of the ball, the gilded members of that generation were obliged to face public ridicule. Their golden boots had turned to lead.

Of the six players highlighted by Lineker (he didn't name them), only one achieved true world class in the six years that linked the lightning strike in Bavaria with that humbling by the Croats. Michael Owen, who scored goals in competitive fixtures against Argentina and Brazil, was undoubtedly a striker of international pedigree before his hamstrings betrayed him. He was no Greaves, but he was very good.

The others shrank in the shirt. Gerrard and Frank Lampard, so commanding for Liverpool and Chelsea, did not justify their star billing. Rio Ferdinand was an elegant defender, so elegant that he appeared to play in a silk dressing gown. Wayne Rooney's immense gifts were liable to evaporate in the steam rising from his ears. As for the sixth member of Lineker's global domination club, one imagines it was David Beckham. Ho hum.

England have known golden generations before. Towards the end of Sir Alf Ramsey's period in office, and in Don Revie's three-year reign, they could have called on Peter Osgood, Tony Currie, Alan Hudson, Charlie George and Frank Worthington, but they rarely did. 'Mavericks', you see. Can't be trusted. Some of those players must look at their successors, who have achieved so little despite their hundreds of caps, and weep. Never has a generation been told how good it is, and failed so dismally. Yet still they were indulged, in the hope that next time things would somehow be 'better'. Meanwhile Greece, from the game's lower reaches, came from nowhere to claim the European Championship in 2004, just as Denmark and Czechoslovakia had taken the prize in previous decades. It just shows what can be achieved.

Noel Coward, a truly golden talent, understood how the wheel turned: 'There's a younger generation knock-knock-knocking at the door.' The Master knew best. When you can't remember your lines, it is wise to leave the stage.

22 Alan Green

Tune into Five Live by day or night, and you will hear Mr Toad in human form. Alan Green sounds so tremendously pleased by the sound of his voice, and the firmness of his convictions, that no agency short of fire, flood or pestilence can prevent him from bestowing his opinions upon the public.

'Next week,' he once informed listeners, in the manner of a flunky drawing up the social diary for minor royals, 'I shall be in Barcelona.' Others went as well, of course. The BBC sports department is not yet a one-man show (though it might be when they up sticks from White City to Salford). Green, who is not the most collegiate of reporters, has no time for such niceties. Listeners want to hear him, and hear him they certainly do.

The crater-faced Ulsterman has talent. He has a clear voice, a reasonable vocabulary, and a willingness to call a spade a shovel. He can reflect the mood of a good game, and has been known to enhance a poor one. His Irishness is also a good thing. There are too many Home Counties boys in the Five Live team, with their pinched tones. So Green is a goal up

before he arrives at the mic. His problem is hogging the ball when a team player would find ways of bringing others into the game.

Here is a man who speaks almost exclusively in capital letters. 'Awful. Disgraceful. Quite Unacceptable.' And that's just at breakfast. His other mode, when he hosts the confederacy of dunces known as *606*, is bafflement, followed by mellifluous suggestion. When listeners approach him to crave a boon, in the manner of peasants petitioning a medieval monarch, he becomes positively unctuous. 'I'll tell you what. D'you know what I think?' Oh, go on, Greeny, tell us what you think. You know you want to.

The glory days of football reporting were dominated by men of a different kidney. Maurice Edleston, Peter Jones and Bryon Butler had clear voices, and recognisable personalities, but did not put themselves between the game and the listener. Although Jones could be a bit soppy ('and Terry Venables smiles that lovely Dagenham smile'), listeners knew they were in safe hands. You got the impression that those men had seen a bit of life beyond the football field.

Then there were the regional specialists: Bill Bothwell on Merseyside, Peter Lorenzo in London, George Bailey in the North East, Larry Canning in the Midlands, and Stuart Hall in Lancashire. Hall's following was boosted by his performances (and, golly, they were performances) on *It's a Knock-Out*, which made him a star of television. He's still going, and still making listeners laugh by refusing to take the game more seriously than a game should be taken.

Hall makes agreeable company on the wireless because he knows that somebody wins, somebody loses, and the caravan moves on. By peppering his match reports with Shakespeare and Shelley he may also have opened a few doors for people who were reluctant to peep inside. Not every presenter welcomed his japes. His 'out' from Boundary Park one wild and windy afternoon was to twist Mark Twain's crack about San Francisco – 'the coldest winter I ever knew was the summer I spent in Oldham'. To which the man in the studio, fooled by Hall's verbal googly, responded: 'I never knew Mark Twain had been to Oldham.' That chap works for Sky now. Lucky Sky.

Twain doesn't feature in the World According to Green. Referees do. He can't get enough of them. 'I hope I won't have to talk about this chap,' he will announce as the game is about to kick off. In that case don't talk about him. But he does, incessantly. Rather like those boggle-eyed folk who deplore pornography, but have to read it to make sure it is deplorable, Green feels he has to talk about the referees who were put on earth to spoil his fun. He talks over the heads of summarisers, too, even when they have something to say. Sometimes he talks about himself more than the men on the field. As often as not, he is wrong, but never is there a suggestion of *mea culpa*.

Selflessness is not essential but it can add a cubit to a person's reputation. Geoffrey Moorhouse dedicated his book on Lord's to John Arlott, who, he wrote, had 'taught millions to appreciate cricket, but has never made the mistake of thinking it the most important thing in life, or of regarding it chiefly as a vehicle for his own performance'.

It is a lovely summation of a man's gifts. It is also a barely veiled rebuke to those reporters who think that sport is the most important thing in life, and that their own performance is necessary to maintain that state of affairs. The outstanding broadcasters have never placed themselves above the games they love. Arlott, for instance, took pains to avoid the first person singular.

Those men are giants of sports reporting. They are men who know their games, and have the humility to serve as witnesses. Green, combative, talented but ultimately ridiculous, considers himself to be a participant in the drama. 'D'you know what I think?' But he doesn't think. Like all bores, he just talks.

23 Alan Hansen

As an accomplished defender for Liverpool and (occasionally) Scotland, Alan Hansen wrote his own reviews. As the BBC's golf-loving pundit-in-chief he goes round in twenty over par. With a face longer than a day without breakfast, he gives a convincing impression of St Jerome in the wilderness. The anchorite did, however, translate the Bible from Greek into Latin, with only a lion for company, so he was entitled to look a bit careworn. Hansen, who sees jokes strictly by appointment, has no excuse for his cussedness.

Humourless, dogmatic, repetitive, Hansen leans on his favourite adjectives like verbal crutches. Everything is either 'un-believable', even when viewers are prepared to accept the evidence of their own eyes, or it is 'incredible', though nobody's credulity has been challenged. When those assertions prove inadequate a player is deemed to have been 'brull-yun', a word he uses to describe anybody who has observed the terms of his contract by turning up. 'Great' is another favourite. He has no ear for language, no aptitude for debate, no critical detachment. You would get more sense out of Archie Andrews.

It has become a bit of a cliché to laugh at the football 'experts' on the box, with a vocabulary that stretches to about thirty words, but there is no reason they have to be so poor. Consider the Irish. John Giles, the star of RTE's coverage, is an outstanding summariser, and although Eamon Dunphy is a bit of a controversialist, there is no doubting his independence. Those men speak clearly, in properly conceived sentences, ignoring the platitudes about players 'being disappointed' and the rest of the verbal flotsam that comes so naturally to pundits on this side of the water. They comment on the game in a disinterested manner. They are not there to tickle the tummies of overrated mummers.

Not for them the BBC habit of referring chummily to players and managers by their given names or nicknames. Nor, it must be said, in the interests of fairness, are ITV any better. The pundits on both channels refer reflexively to England as 'we', in the manner of cheerleaders without pom-poms. Woe betide anybody who rocks the boat.

In this pushmi-pullyu world there are occasional moments of levity. Peter Reid, unaccountably invited to bolster the BBC team, once informed viewers that England would 'batter' Macedonia, and liked the verb so much that he took it home at the end of the evening. It was about the only word he used that was intelligible. The Beeb should have run subtitles that night to translate what the catarrhal Liverpudlian was trying to say. Macedonia were well and truly battered, by the way, scoring twice in a game of four goals.

These days people tend to giggle at the mention of Jimmy Hill, which is a shame. At his best, Hill brought a genuine curiosity to the pundit's role. He may not have enjoyed Hansen's success as a player but his record over the past fifty years reveals him to be a man who has given the professional game at least as much as the former Liverpool star.

It was Hill, as chairman of the Professional Footballers' Association, who fought a noble battle with Cliff Lloyd, the union's secretary, to remove players from the yoke of servitude. In 1961 they won a court ruling that overturned the maximum wage that kept players in their place. Then, as a pioneering young manager of Coventry City, he took them into the First Division. So when he went into punditry, first at London Weekend Television, then at the BBC, he was well equipped to shine as an eloquent and – in the best sense – provocative expert. Unlike Hansen, whose eyes can glaze over when others hold the floor, he also listened to his fellows.

The golden age of punditry came at the very start. The World Cup of 1970 brought together on ITV the conflicting voices of the youthful Brian Clough, Derek Dougan, Malcolm Allison and Pat Crerand. What would a producer today give for such a quartet? Not much, in all probability. The modern urge for the safe, measured and known might well count against those strong personalities, who were capable of expressing sharp opinions in vivid language. 'The Germans do it,' a perplexed Mike Channon once told the studio. 'The French do it.' In jumped Clough with 'even educated fleas do it!' It was the sort of witty, unscripted remark that never springs from the lips of Hansen and company.

Gary Lineker, with his talk of 'har-larts', is a capable presenter, though he has been given more opportunities to 'train on' than less favoured horses in the television stable who did not share his playing background. But it is hard to find many kind words for Alan Shearer, a fine centre forward in his day, or Mark Lawrenson, a splendid defender. Despite his fondness for merry quips, Lawrenson should not be pointed in the direction of Blackpool's south pier.

Playing the game, however well, is not the same as commenting on it. When Hansen served Liverpool so nimbly, Brian Glanville called him 'an elegant giver of second chances'. With that pithy, wounding phrase he revealed greater wit, not to say a closer understanding of the game, than Hansen has managed in a decade of sugar-coated banalities. But Glanville is a journalist.

The best writers have always made more sense of events than players, most of whom observe the professional's code of *omerta* long after they have put their boots in the attic. Other sports have truth-tellers. Cricket has Geoffrey Boycott. Rugby has Stuart Barnes. Tennis has John McEnroe. They are not to all tastes. Some people cannot bear to listen. But they provide grit in the oyster. Football has Alan Hansen, who has nothing to say and is determined to say it.

24 Derek Hatton

The tragic events at the Heysel Stadium, Brussels, in May 1985, when Liverpool met Juventus in the final of the European Cup, can be traced back to the final played in Rome the year before. On that occasion, when their team beat Roma on penalties, Liverpool supporters were attacked by some of the notorious hooligans who make the Eternal City such an unwelcoming place for outsiders.

They can be traced back, certainly, but what took place in Brussels that night cannot be excused by the anger of the fans who remembered what had happened twelve months previously. The facts are simple and damning. After a violent charge across the terracing before the match by Liverpool fans, many of them high on drink, thirty-nine supporters of the Italian club lost their lives. The final went ahead, Juventus winning 1–0, but it was the last football any English club side played in Europe for five years. Liverpool, who had won the European Cup four times in nine seasons before 'Heysel', as it came to be known, served an additional year's punishment.

The revulsion felt throughout the continent ran deep, and in Turin the wounds have never healed. When Liverpool played

Juventus in the European Cup twenty-three years later many Italian fans who travelled to Anfield turned their backs, literally as well as metaphorically, on their hosts. They had not forgotten the dead, just as Liverpool's fans will not forget the ninety-six who lost their lives at Hillsborough in 1989. For people in Italy, and beyond, what happened that awful night was merely the last, grotesque enactment of a ritual that had, in the previous decade, left all of Europe besmirched in a trail of blood and broken glass.

In Liverpool there was a sense of shame. There was also a man who felt he could bring together the people of two battered cities. Derek Hatton, a fireman who had become the deputy leader of Liverpool City Council, had begun to make a reputation on the national stage as a strutting peacock of the far left, and the so-called 'peace mission' he led to Turin brought more headlines.

In Hatton's estimation, Liverpool and Turin were working-class cities united in grief. United they were, through a night in infamy, though the grief was not distributed equally. It never can be when one city is busy burying its dead, and the other is covering its head in disgrace. It appeared an unseemly intrusion, as Liverpool's two bishops were invited to swell the city delegation, and the years have not bestowed dignity on Hatton's unlikely jaunt.

Twenty-first-century readers have a clear-eyed witness to help them understand the events that unfolded after Heysel. Ian Jack, the writer and journalist, wrote a superb account of the ill-conceived 'mission' in *The Sunday Times* magazine that has entered the annals of reportage. His observations (and they were observations: he visited both cities in a spirit of genuine inquiry) shone a light that still shines.

Considering Hatton's claim that Liverpool and Turin were working-class cities united in grief, Jack found two places that could hardly be more different. In terms of relative wealth, he wrote, Liverpool resembled Calabria, in the poverty-ravaged heel of Italy, while Turin enjoyed a standard of living comparable to that of the Home Counties. Nor was the distinction one solely of economic status. Jack found, as has many a writer before him, that Italians of all classes want to eat well, drink well, dress well; live well. Watching an Italian family prepare the evening meal, he could see in his mind's eye the tatty corner shops back in Liverpool where people dutifully bought their tins of beans. He heard the docker's daughter, granted an education her father had been denied, speaking roughly in order not to sound posh.

Jack's piece opened the eyes of some British readers to different worlds of feeling and being. It brought to mind the words of Anthony Burgess, one of those writers who, since the days of Keats, have been bewitched by Italy. 'In England,' he wrote, 'art turns no wheels, it bakes no bread.' For art, read life. Jack's act of witness exposed Hatton's comparison. Whether Hatton felt any shame was immaterial. To judge by his public utterances before he was finally routed by an outraged Neil Kinnock at a Labour Party conference some years later, and kicked out of the party, shame was not a word that featured in his vocabulary. Now, to nobody's great surprise, he is an all-round entrepreneur and property developer.

Like other English cities, Liverpool has changed considerably in the past quarter-century. There are bars galore, hotels aplenty, and 'leisure facilities' on every street corner. Yet, as with other English cities, evidence of Burgess's wheel-turning and bread-baking is hard to find. Even the honour of being a European City of Culture in 2008 (a case of Buggins' Turn) failed to change many perceptions of the city. How could it, when a city spokesman boasted that one of the year's highlights was an exhibition devoted to Gustav Klimt, the Viennese painter, 'who was bling – and Liverpool is bling'. Read, and weep! The English, in their ugly modern guise, are rampant consumers. They are not great discriminators. Indeed, discrimination has become a naughty word. It implies making judgements, and we wouldn't want that, would we?

Hatton, an Everton fan as it happens, had used football to hitch a ride. He was a crowd-pleasing politician and by hanging on to the coat-tails of the 'people's game', which had dealt Liverpool such a grievous blow, he hoped to score a goal for the city in the dock of public opinion. The public beyond Liverpool was not prepared to listen. As anybody could have told him, a hearse makes a poor bandwaggon.

25 Nigel Kennedy

When sufficient time has passed, another fifty years or so, social historians may look back on English life in the last decades of the twentieth century and wonder why the middle class had such a death wish. People who were raised in certain ways sought to renounce their inheritance. All they did was undermine the institutions that had nursed them.

In many cases mild regret turned into self-abasement. Men and women (usually men) let it be known they were ashamed of their background, and even their nationality. They had been educated at private schools but hadn't 'agreed' with that kind of thing. Many had gone on to ancient universities, but would prefer not to have done. They lived in big houses but cared deeply for the less fortunate, and would talk of little else when their friends, who had been to similar schools and lived in houses which looked much the same, popped round for some couscous and Rioja. Despite this play-acting, it didn't stop them schooling their children in places where they pretended to have been so unhappy. Labour politicians, with time-honoured dishonesty, proved particularly fond of private education.

Naturally, some of these social reformers changed the way they spoke. RP was out and bogus proletarian voices were in, because that was how 'real' people talked. In a moment of supreme idiocy, that may prove so useful for those social historians, Liz Forgan declared upon taking over as managing director of BBC Radio that she was longing to hear 'those beautiful Brummie accents'. Within the BBC, where such attitudes grew like pond life, her comments were considered unremarkable.

A prime example of this bizarre social transformation is Nigel Kennedy. A brilliant child violinist, Kennedy was a hot-house flower, born to a cello-playing father in Sussex by the sea. He attended the school for musicians in Surrey established by Yehudi Menuhin, who, sensing that he might have landed a big fish, kept a close eye on the young Kennedy. Menuhin's aim was to stimulate the intellectual curiosity of the young, not just get them to practise their scales. There is BBC footage from those days which reveals Kennedy to be a well-spoken Home Counties child, as one might expect.

He remained well spoken until, in his late twenties, he lapsed into a delayed adolescence. He adopted a silly 'mockney' voice, augmented by verbal padding, and introduced significant . . . pauses . . . in . . . his . . . conversation to suggest that he was . . . like . . . searching for something . . . meaningful to say. He began to swear in interviews, which is never a good sign. He spoke of 'digging' jazz and hanging out with 'cats', which would have sounded absurd in the Chicago of the 1950s, never mind London four decades later. He dropped his Christian name, to sound 'cool'. He collaborated with unsuitable partners. In short he behaved like a twerp.

Naturally this period of 'growing down' coincided with an oft-expressed passion for football. Hardly an interview passed without Kennedy drawing attention to the unremarkable fact that he supported Aston Villa. Yes, it was Kennedy the celebrity fan! He painted his Jaguar in the club's claret and blue colours, and took to performing the theme tune from *Match of the Day* as a party piece, to show he was a man of the people, not some stuck-up snob who had passed through a college of knowledge.

In 1990 he followed the England team to the World Cup in Italy, where he passed himself off as a bit of a character: hey diddle diddle, the cat with the fiddle! Isaac Stern, one of Kennedy's mentors when he studied at the Juilliard School in New York, once serenaded Jimmy Connors at the US Open, but here was a young man scraping away for Queen and country. Good boy!

There have been other celebrity fans. Elton John, whose love of the game was genuine, became chairman of Watford, and Eric Morecambe was a director of Luton Town. Delia Smith, elevated to the chair at Norwich City, took to the pitch one night at Carrow Road to tell fans, 'Let's be having you!' Stars of the pop world are regular fans. Ray Davies and Roger Daltrey follow Arsenal, and Robert Plant has watched Wolves all his life. Moving a few notches down the scale, the ghastly Gallagher brothers support Manchester City.

You expect folk from the pop and film world to take an interest. Kennedy is different because the nature of his support was a clear case of special pleading. 'Look at me, I'm normal.' Happily, his musical talents remained unimpaired when he trusted them. Not playing the jazz he took such a shine to, but the proper classical stuff he affected to mistrust. He made his name with the Elgar concerto, the last of the great romantic works for his instrument, and recorded it twice, proving that, while he might talk nonsense, he played none when the mood took him.

The connection with the great composer is instructive. Elgar was also a football fan, cycling from his home in Worcestershire to watch Wolves play at Molineux. Yet how different the men were, and what a gulf in social attitudes separated them.

Unlike Kennedy, who had been groomed for a life in music from the moment he could walk, Elgar was an outsider four times over as a self-taught, lower-middle-class, provincial Catholic. His wife's father, a general, thought his daughter had married beneath her station, and snubbed them. It took Elgar more than four decades to become an overnight sensation with *Enigma Variations* in 1899, but ended up with a knighthood, an OM, a baronetcy and an imperishable place in the life of his country. And not once did he affect a silly accent, or dress down, to persuade others of his 'street cred'.

Elgar's innocent love of football and the turf was an extension of his personality. Kennedy's obsession came across as an assumption of a role he felt obliged to play: the common man. He has calmed down a bit now, and is better for it. But it was a close-run thing.

26 Richard Keys

In his superb book about English drinking, *Beer and Skittles*, Richard Boston made a distinction between a pub and a bar. There can be no precise definition, for the two sometimes overlap, but he got closer than most. A pub, he said, offered those who supped there a retreat; it created its own world. A bar was an extension of the street.

Boston would have gone along with that great Englishman, Dr Johnson, who thought that a good inn, with good ale and good company, offered mankind more happiness than just about anything else. It is an English invention, which cannot be replicated elsewhere, no matter how hard people try. The 'English pub' in California or the Western Cape, with its olde worlde name, chilled keg beer and rubbery fish and chips, is not the same thing as a proper English pub.

Yet, each week, in city and hamlet, the English pub is losing its identity. The old names are going, as the Three Horseshoes becomes Bar Vegas, or something equally daft, in an attempt to attract the young, who must be indulged at all times, to satisfy the advertisers. With the names go the customs that sustained those pubs through decades of happy quaffing, and the toothsome local ales that were the glory of English brewing.

Since 1992 there has been another curse on the pub: Sky Television. Few sights crush the spirits quite so thoroughly as the promise, spelt out on large, colourful banners outside a thousand hostelries, that drinkers can watch sport LIVE tonight, tomorrow night, every blessed night. And by sport the pub is really talking about football, in all its guises. For millions of English people, who are not interested in watching football, the pub is no longer a haven of innocent recreation, it is a place to be avoided.

Some of the pubs that offer live football are not, it is true, places the curious drinker would enter willingly. That is no great loss. But there is little doubt that the tone of our town pubs has altered significantly since Sky showered gold sovereigns into the lap of Premier League bigwigs in 1992. Exclusive rights to live action made Rupert Murdoch even richer. In time it also made Richard Keys the face of Sky Sport.

For a man who possesses few qualities that viewers traditionally value in their broadcasters, Keys has done very well. He has the sort of voice that is more commonly heard reading out badminton results at the local rec, and a chummy manner ('Jamie's with us again') that falls a few furlongs short of authority. But that is what his masters want: a nonentity, who can be relied upon to tell white lies. At all times he must stay 'on message' and the message could not be more simple: on Sky football is always wonderful.

This is no David Coleman or Des Lynam, who had strong

screen personalities. He is not even a Jim Rosenthal, an able all-rounder with a pleasing smile. Nearly two decades into his role Keys comes over as a malleable, one-dimensional chap who is doing the job during the vac until the big boys return, full of vim and vigour, from their Tuscan adventures.

The obsequious lightweight should not carry the can for Sky's coverage. Murdoch and his henchmen, Sam Chisholm and David Hill, rewrote the book on sports broadcasting. But, as the most visible symbol of their coverage, the one who sets up the studio experts ('Big Sam has joined us tonight'), he has become a fixture in televised sport. Suit, tie, coathanger smile, bran-tub of clichés. All present and correct. Off we jolly well go.

As for the coverage, it is uncritical enough to have been scripted by a Russian commissar of agriculture who has just received the latest figures on grain production. The players are there to be petted, and joshed with ('Stevie G is with us – you were in fine form tonight, Stevie'), until, in the fullness of time, they can swell the ranks of the recently retired in the studio, where Keys will lap up their ungrammatical 'expertise' with the ease of a man whose purpose in life is to be deferential.

The result of this endless verbal smooching is the lionisation of second-raters. Just as Larkin satirised the complacent attitudes of the Sixties by writing that 'sexual intercourse began in 1963', a generation has grown up believing that English football really did begin in 1992, after the big bang generated by Murdoch's moolah. Billions of pounds later it is considered impolite to point out that, while many people have become significantly richer, neither the quality of football throughout the four divisions, nor the coverage of the game has improved.

Sky stands supreme. It has mastered the useless graphic, the pointless soundtrack (the louder the better), and all the other appurtenances of television gimmickry that have ruined a thousand pubs. And, in the middle of it all, wearing his toothpaste smile, assuring us that we are going to watch something wonderful, Bolton Wanderers playing Stoke City LIVE!!! – who could possibly want to be doing anything else – sits a man in a suit delighted to be talking to his good pals, Master Redknapp and Big Sam, reminding viewers that every day, in every way, things get better and better.

27 Lord Kinnaird

We owe the Victorians much more than we are sometimes prepared to let on. They founded schools for the poor and hospitals for the sick, established libraries and museums to educate all, and forged a national system of railways. Propelled by a sense of civic duty, reflected in public buildings that still look magnificent, they lived through an age of unparalleled prosperity. As Europe became enmeshed in various revolutions, Britain stood supreme.

Lytton Strachey may have begun the debunking process with his book, *Eminent Victorians*, but it really was an age of heroic figures, grand gestures. Think of Matthew Arnold, author of *Culture and Anarchy*. What wouldn't we give now for some 'sweetness and light', and 'the best that has been thought and said'? But who needs an agency of personal transformation when we can luxuriate in the hot tub of *Britain's Got Talent*?

The Victorians brought us the idea of muscular Christianity, which was the seedbed of professional sport. And there is much to be said for *mens sana in corpore sano*, which was not a Victorian idea, though it could well have been. More specifically it was one of the social engines that drove the great public schools, like the Rugby of Thomas Arnold, father of the great Matthew.

There is, naturally, another side to the inventory. In *Tom Brown's Schooldays*, the famous fictional re-creation of Rugby by Thomas Hughes, readers are introduced to Flashman, an out-and-out rotter. But he was a rotter it was easy to admire on the sly. How else could George MacDonald Fraser have fashioned a sequence of best-selling novels based on Flashman's imagined post-Rugby exploits a century later?

In real life there were also a few rotters, one of whom played a significant part in the development of Association Football. Arthur, Lord Kinnaird, born in 1847, was a tackler of such well-known vigour that he was celebrated as king of the 'hackers'. After one particularly physical encounter his mother was alarmed that, one day, he might come home with a broken leg. 'If he does,' said a friend, 'it won't be his own.'

Kinnaird, Eton and Cambridge, was an FA Cup winner five times, three times with Wanderers, twice with the Old Etonians. In all he appeared in nine finals, and played for Scotland against England in 1873. So the noble lord with the bushy red beard may be seen as the first exponent of physical engagement that has subsequently carried the reputation of English football across the globe. We have rarely produced great players, but our game has always revelled in extreme physicality. To this day one of the most common shouts of encouragement (or implied criticism) is: 'Get stuck in!'

Some players have been more decorous than others. The Bolton full-back pairing of Roy Hartle and Tommy Banks earned a fearsome reputation in the Fifties. Banks, who played six times for England, once shouted at Hartle, who had been beastly to some hapless winger: 'When you've finished with him, chip him over here.' Hartle's tackling was reckoned to be even more ferocious. It was Hartle, faced with the prospect of containing Tom Finney, who told the great winger: 'You can push the ball past me, Tom, and you can run past me, but you're not going together.'

Banks and Hartle were, from all available evidence, manly players, not dirty ones. Their successors in spirit include Nobby Stiles, despite the clobbering he gave Jackie Simon of France in the 1966 World Cup, and Stuart Pearce, a genuinely hard player who had no sense of malice. One might, if one felt charitable, add the names of Norman Hunter and Tommy Smith, tough-tackling defenders from the Sixties, though the men they played against knew that the defender they all bounced off was Bobby Moore. Inside that velvet cloak there was a body of granite.

In recent years standards have dropped off alarmingly. Paul Ince, a middle-ranking midfielder, liked to present himself as 'the guv'nor', but few people endorsed his martial qualities. Many laughed at his effrontery. Towards the end of his career, when he was playing indifferently at Anfield, unable to raise much of a gallop, one member of the press box observed disdainfully: 'How kind of Liverpool to erect a statue to Paul Ince in the centre circle.'

For many modern English footballers tackling is a mysterious craft, undertaken with some trepidation. A fair amount of hacking still goes on, though not the robust type favoured by Lord Kinnaird and his titled pals, for whom an exchange of bracing challenges in heavy leather boots was a prelude to a hearty dinner. The modern hacker is a sly chap, who goes in for a more covert form of skulduggery. Cast your eye over the villains of the Premier League. We're not talking about gentlemen. Compared with Hartle or Pearce, most are mardy boys.

Kinnaird the Anglo-Scot was a gentleman all right. A muscular Christian gentleman. He was president of the YMCA in England, a director of Barclays Bank, and Lord High Commissioner to the General Assembly of the Church of Scotland. Not a rotter at all, really. He was another of those remarkable Victorians who gave us so much. For better or worse, the formidable hacker left an indelible mark upon the game as well as opponents. Even if his legacy helped to foul up the game, he was quite a chap.

28 Nick Love

'There are those who go down to the sewers to bathe,' wrote Ibsen, the father of modern drama. 'I go there to purify.' It is a fine distinction, and would be lost on many of those who consider themselves to be 'artists' in our world. One can think of a few daubers of paint who might not recognise the playwright's truism. It would certainly baffle Nick Love, whose 2004 film, *The Football Factory*, was the most murky contribution so far to the treatment of the hooligans who have blighted football.

Go to a decent bookshop, and in the sports section you will find a shelf devoted to football hooliganism, and the supposed motivation of the people who commit violence. To borrow a phrase that used to be applied to French philosophers, there is no act so foul that an English sociologist cannot be prevailed upon to excuse it. Or, one might add, a film-maker with an idea to pitch. Love based his horrible movie on a book by John King which concerned the rival 'firms' of Millwall and Chelsea. The result was a nauseous brew of violence and drug-taking, dressed up as an exercise in social realism. Those who lasted the course, and did not walk out in disgust, needed to take a long shower afterwards.

There is no law that says good films cannot be made about bad people. Martin Scorsese, to mention only the most obvious example, has fashioned a successful career out of portraying men of violence. (In his quest for cinematic substance, Love borrowed, as an homage, one scene directly from *GoodFellas* for *The Football Factory*, and failed miserably.) But to make a film work, there must be some detachment between director and subject. Although Scorsese has often been accused of being half in love with something his films are intended to deplore, he has never knowingly bathed in the sewer. His best films bear the stamp of a modern master.

Love, by contrast, made no attempt to put any distance between his lens and the *untermenschen* who filled the screen. So the film, tainted by narcissism, and overlaid with self-pity, lacked a moral compass. Poorly written and acted, even though real-life hooligans were roped in to lend some 'authenticity', it did not find an audience among the platoons of social misfits it sought to lionise as misunderstood youths (and others not so young). It was a total failure, as was *The Yank*, an improbable film about a Harvard drop-out joining a bunch of West Ham thugs (as so many Ivy Leaguers do).

In his attempts to bump it up, however, Love revealed the kind of sloppy thinking that continues to damage football. The film, he said, was not really about thugs hitting one another. It was about friendship and loyalty. Well, after a fashion it was, just as the Nuremberg rallies affirmed a corporate identity. Hiding behind one of those generalisations with which the ignorant try to block tunnels of thought, he thought it showed 'the nation's dissatisfaction with Blair's Britain'. There were many things that could be laid at the door of our erstwhile Prime Minister. That was not one of them.

Nor had Love finished. His film, he said, was about 'passion, heroics, the recounting of battles. It's uniquely British, and is apparently endlessly fascinating to the rest of the world.' He made it sound a bit like *Brief Encounter* meets *Chitty Chitty Bang Bang*! How could anybody resist?

Oddly enough, 'the rest of the world' did just that. Perhaps many of them were too familiar with their first-hand experiences of young Englishmen on their travels in search of cheap beer, cheap drugs and lashings of sex and violence. As for heroics and the recounting of battles, the genuinely heroic men who lived through two World Wars took care, in the main, not to boast of their exploits, even though they had much to brag about. The briefest look at any of the thousands of obituaries which celebrated their lives would have informed the dimmest of the dim that most of them slipped quietly back into civilian life without so much as a word about what they had done. Heroes, as a rule, do not seek opportunities to reveal acts of heroism. They would rather be playing dominos in the snug, or pruning their roses.

But this is to take our film-maker more seriously than he deserves. It is better to observe that, in the week before his film came out, a Birmingham teacher was convicted and jailed for helping to organise a fight between supporters of Charlton Athletic and Southampton. Clearly, he was one of those unfortunates that Mr Blair had failed.

We haven't heard much of Love since he made his grubby film, and he hasn't been missed. But should you see somebody floundering in a dirty pool near your home, bleating about the injustices of society, do not feel obliged to pull him out.

29 Steve McClaren

Even when he wears an expensive suit Steve McClaren has the shifty look of a poacher who has a rabbit tucked under his coat, and is trying to dodge the gamekeeper. It is the look of somebody who fears he is in the wrong place and, during his unhappy period as manager of England, that judgement was widely shared.

McClaren was never expected to succeed Sven-Goran Eriksson. Brian Barwick, the chief executive of the Football Association, turned to him only after he had been rebuffed by Luis Felipe Scolari, the manager of Portugal, who had initially shown some interest in the post. When Scolari, a World Cup winner with Brazil, withdrew his candidacy, Barwick pushed the claims of the Middlesbrough manager, despite the fact that not one member of the interviewing panel spoke in his favour. It was the ultimate committee decision, and brought consequences that surprised few.

With Scolari a non-runner the race should have gone to Martin O'Neill, the sharp-witted Irishman. Instead, in their eagerness to promote an English coach, the wise men appointed Eriksson's assistant, who had done or said little to suggest he

had the making of an international manager. He lasted sixteen months. A 3–2 defeat at Wembley by Croatia in November 2007, when a draw would have sufficed, meant that England would play no part in the finals of the European Championship. McClaren cleared out his desk the next morning.

That sodden evening at Wembley supplied an unflattering final image of McClaren. As the Croatians gave his players a lesson in the deceptively simple art of passing the ball, the manager sheltered under his umbrella. It was his Gene Kelly moment, only without the song and dance. 'The wally with a brolly', ran a headline, which, without being terribly funny, summed up a miserable night. McClaren looked forlorn, a man without friends or hope.

It was his vigorous attempt to make friends that helped to bring him down. No sooner had he assumed Eriksson's job in July 2006 than he approached Max Clifford, the public-relations consultant, for advice. It was the decision of a weak man. Confident men do not let on that their armour can be pierced so easily, though they do listen to others when circumstances alter.

Until then McClaren had been spared the spotlight. He made a name (of sorts) for himself as a coach at Derby County, and when Sir Alex Ferguson invited him to become his assistant at Old Trafford in 1999 they immediately landed the famous treble of Premier League, FA Cup and Champions League. Or rather, Ferguson landed the triple prize. McClaren watched, and learned.

Two years later he was off to Middlesbrough, where he took them to the League Cup in 2004. It was the club's first significant trophy and, coupled with his coaching duties under Eriksson, it made him an outsider for the post when the Swede shuffled off. And an outsider he should have remained.

The liaison with Clifford, a high-profile operator, was never likely to bear fruit. Clifford called time on the arrangement after four months, claiming that he did not have sufficient access to his client. What did he expect, a berth in the dressing-room? Still, McClaren's teeth were gleaming by then, so he got something from the deal.

Colgate Steve made other poor decisions. He dropped David Beckham, quite rightly, and then restored him to the squad for no reason other than that Beckham was a big name. He preferred Wes Brown and Ledley King as defenders to Jamie Carragher, who was in the form of his life at Liverpool. Carragher announced his retirement from international football.

Here was a man who palpably could not get the best out of his players. Sometimes he could not get the best out of himself. In October 2006 it was his plan to toddle off to America, to spend time with the Seattle Seahawks NFL team: to what purpose nobody really knew. In the end a 2–0 defeat by Croatia in Zagreb pulled the plug on that adventure, but it did leave people wondering what McClaren thought he was up to.

Desperate times require desperate measures, so McClaren called up Terry Venables as his assistant. It was a last throw of the dice. As the European Championship campaign rolled on McClaren clung on to his authority like Humphrey Bogart in *The Caine Mutiny*. He had lost the confidence of those close to him, and had never enjoyed the backing of the football public, who could hardly believe his appointment in the first place.

It was a very English balls-up, for which neither Barwick nor anybody else privy to the decision ever took full responsibility. Here was a moderate manager, not remotely equipped for the perils of international management, promoted in order to give 'our guys' a go. In short, it was a shambles.

McClaren was a club manager, no more. In June 2008 he accepted an offer from FC Twente in Holland to be their coach, and became a figure of fun at once when he assumed a cod 'Dutch' accent in a television interview in which he talked about his side being 'underdogsh'! He reached the Dutch Cup Final, where Twente lost on penalties. It was the story of his career: not good enough.

30 Freddie Mercury

It is touching to see nobility in victory. Regrettably the small gestures of acknowledgement seem to be a thing of the past. The batsman who used to touch his cap on reaching a century is now more likely to wave his bat around like a scythe at hay-making. The rugby player who dives to score an important try flings the ball skywards and waves at his friends in the crowd rather than trotting back to his own half in the approved manner.

We shouldn't be too starchy about celebrations. When Marco Tardelli scored Italy's second goal in the 1982 World Cup Final, to ensure they would beat the Germans, he tore round the field like a wild thing, and everybody was happy for him. Here was a marvellous player scoring a terrific goal in the World Cup Final, and behaving in an exuberant manner that was absolutely in character. It was one of football's great moments.

The English have traditionally mistrusted overt displays of emotion. We like to remember Bobby Moore preparing to collect the World Cup from the Queen at Wembley in 1966 as a captain of his country should. Is my shirt tucked in? Are my hands clean? Do I look presentable? Very well, I shall proceed to meet Her Majesty. Moore's performance after the final, no less than his performance during it, was also one of the great moments. Here was a man from a humble background who wore his captain's robes with the dignity of a prince.

Expectations have changed, and how. These days, no sooner has a team won a trophy than a hundred rockets go off, the sound system is turned up full blast, and players are encouraged to bounce up and down for the benefit of the great god television, which has paid handsomely for the spectacle, and is going to get its money's worth. Even Moore might have had to shake a leg in our multi-media age, or roar something suitably triumphant into a camera.

Oh dear, that coarse triumphalism. There is no need for false modesty when you can boast 'We are the champions', which brings us to Freddie Mercury. An exotic bird of a pop singer, dead before his time of AIDS, he contributed the most horrible element to the undignified modern victory rite. 'We are the Champions', Queen's hit of 1977, has become a Radetzky March for two generations of excitable victors. Every time a winner is unveiled, Mercury is reborn in his leather pants to tell us he has 'no time for losers, 'cos we are the champions of the WOOOORLD!'

Camp as a hill of tents, this prancing queen was a bit of a joke, as were Queen themselves. How else can one describe a group who sang about 'fat-bottomed girls' and whose most famous hit, 'Bohemian Rhapsody', ranks alongside 'Imagine' as the worst pop song ever written? 'Imagine no possessions,' crooned Jolly Jack Lennon, who certainly couldn't imagine a world without them. A month after that record was released he put his Surrey mansion on the market for £175,000, millions in today's terms. Power to the people!

Football crowds have always appropriated pop songs. The Beatles gave the terraces 'Hey Jude', which was amended according to circumstances. Bob Dylan's 'Mighty Quinn', given a lick of paint by Manfred Mann, was picked up by Liverpool supporters to serenade Emlyn Hughes, and Manchester City fans borrowed from the Small Faces songbook to croak 'sha la la la Summerbee'. The Kinks were not ignored. Red-baiters everywhere used to bowdlerise 'Dead End Street': 'What are we living for? To see Man Utd in division four!'

Since then other hits have entered the repertoire but the most popular songwriter with football fans is, to nobody's surprise, the most famous songwriter of the twentieth century. 'You simply must work with Dick Rodgers,' Noel Coward told a lyricist who had been invited to break bread with the King of Broadway. 'He pees melody.' Rodgers wrote a greater number of soaring tunes than anybody, living or dead, and two of them are sung, indifferently it is true, every week of the football season: 'You'll Never Walk Alone' and 'Blue Moon'. Oscar Hammerstein wrote the words for the first song, Lorenz Hart for the second. Rodgers, who liked to count his pennies, tried to claim royalties when he heard that Liverpool supporters had appropriated his anthem from *Carousel*!

'We are the Champions' was different. With its vainglorious lyrics and laboured melody, it was written with the football terraces in mind. It has no place in the great popular songbook but, sung in an earnest way by little Freddie, who gave the impression that he was baring his soul for his art, it can serve as a most effective laxative. It's a quite horrible record, a mephitic eruption of flatulence, released by an absurd man in a moment of such ripe self-parody that even Norma Desmond in her Hollywood grotto might have blushed for shame.

Mercury, brave chap, went on to perform a preposterous 'opera' duet with Montserrat Caballe. She wore the trousers.

31 Piers Morgan

When England beat West Germany on that sun-kissed day in July 1966, thousands of Germans stood alongside the England supporters at Wembley. There were no songs about RAF bombers strafing German cities, no Nazi salutes. The Second World War was fresh in the memory, and the brave men and women who survived it knew that the magnificent fighting spirit of the Wehrmacht would be put to more productive use in peacetime. The German economic miracle surprised few.

Thirty years later, when the teams met at Wembley for a place in the final of the European Championship, the mood had changed. It was now permissible, indeed almost compulsory, to bait Brother Hun for a bit of a laugh. All that was needed was a volunteer. Up went the hand of Piers Pughe Morgan, an impulsive, quick-witted chap with a showman's instincts, who had moved swiftly through the ranks in Fleet Street. Starting as a gossip-hound on the *Sun* he had risen, by way of the *News of the World*, to edit the *Mirror*.

In its glory days the *Mirror* had been damned by the great columnist, Bernard Levin, as 'a repository of bogus radicalism'.

Those days were long gone. Old Labour by temperament, read by the last representatives of a working class that no longer existed, the paper now went in for occasional gags, in an attempt to outdo the 'currant bun'. The front page of 25 June 1996 came straight from a comic book: 'Achtung! Surrender'. Morgan mocked up pictures of England players wearing pith helmets, ho ho, to add a touch of, what, irony? An Englischer joke, ja? But nobody was laughing when hundreds of English fans, full of beer and resentment after Germany's victory, forced police officers to seal off Trafalgar Square. To the bewilderment of tourists wandering home from a night in the West End the fans ran wild, smashing the windows of any German car that happened to be in the area.

As Morgan had never really left the froth-and-bubble world from which he emerged, and to which he has returned with an enthusiasm that is rather unnerving, it is possible that the infamous front page was dreamt up after-hours in a Soho club, where many an editorial decision has been hatched in convivial circumstances. Whatever the provenance, it was a calculated insult to a friendly nation, and the football team that represented it. A football team, it hardly needs saying, that has been significantly more successful down the decades than England's, and there's the rub.

There are pretty obvious reasons why Brazil, Italy and Argentina are better than England. They produce players who are more comfortable on the ball, and have a wider range of skills. Most countries produce more gifted players than the English. Sometimes the gulf in class is oceanic: think of the

French teams led by Michel Platini and Zinedine Zidane, and Johan Cruyff's Hollanders. Most countries except, funnily enough, the Germans, which is where the envy comes in.

Other than the great XI led by Franz Beckenbauer that won the European Championship in 1972, a side even finer than the one that went on to win the World Cup two years later, the Germans have not necessarily had better players than England. Some obviously stand out. Beckenbauer, Gunter Netzer, Paul Breitner and Gerd Muller would have adorned any team. Even when Netzer lost form, they could bring back a midfielder like Wolfgang Overath. There have been others: Bernd Schuster, Karl-Heinz Rummenigge, Jurgen Klinsmann, Lothar Matthaeus, Matthias Sammer. But on the whole the Germans and the English have been pretty evenly matched in talent, if not character. Yet Fritz continues to quaff the pilsner of champions while Dusty Miller goes home to bread and water.

The inequality of outcome goes a bit beyond the cliché of 'Teutonic efficiency' propounded by so many pundits. That's right, the 'efficiency' that gave the world Durer, Bach, Beethoven, Goethe, Heine, Kant, Hegel and more mathematicians and physicists than you can shake a stick at! For a people who were so close to us for so long, Germany is a strange land to the modern English. We seem to have forgotten all we ever knew about them, which is why we end up with grubby front-page headlines, passed off as jokes, that reinforce our ignorance. The Germans, who are a more tolerant bunch than we give them credit for, forgive us because, *mirabile dictu*, they like us. Most of the time, at any rate.

In Germany, where they have kept down the price of admission to Bundesliga matches, and where clubs will not countenance ownership by millionaire interlopers, they recognise the importance of producing their own players because they consider the national side to be the single most important element of the game. The *ding-an-sich*, one might say, echoing one of those 'efficient' philosophers. So Germany, who have won three World Cups, and appeared in seven finals, will still be winning them years hence, while England, awash with all that lovely lolly, yet producing few world-class players, will be wondering where all the flowers have gone.

Morgan did not pay for that lapse of judgement with his job, but he was eventually unseated after making another error. Since then he has eagerly embraced the celebrity life he craved/despised so much. Fame eludes him because true fame is determined by achievement, and he is merely a television personality; one of many. As Clive James pointed out in a scintillating radio essay that amounted to a public spanking, Morgan really ought to keep a recording of Beethoven's Seventh Symphony close to hand, to remind himself what real achievement is.

Despite his folly, or possibly because of it, the Germans had the last laugh, as they usually do. Having won the semi-final on penalties (though England played jolly well), they beat the Czech Republic to confirm their third European Championship, and flew home to parade their prize to supporters who expected no less. Before leaving London they took time to place a full-page ad in a broadsheet newspaper, congratulating England on running a fine tournament.

That's the way to do it!

32 Jose Mourinho

It is difficult to predict which players will make good managers. The game is chock-full of outstanding performers who appeared to have what it takes to move seamlessly into management, yet failed. Billy Bremner, Alan Ball and Bryan Robson, to pluck three names from the recent past, were fabled captains of great clubs, but they struggled when it was their turn to pick the team.

Some of the best managers, Sir Alex Ferguson being a case in point, were 'not-quite' as players. Ferguson had a good career, but he wasn't quite good enough to play well at the top level. Another not-quiter was Brian Clough, a formidable goalscorer in the Second Division, who was robbed by injury of the chance to build a stellar career. Possibly it was disappointment that drove them on.

One of the most intriguing trends of recent years has been the emergence of outstanding managers who hardly had playing careers worthy of the name. Rafael Benitez, who took Liverpool to the Champions League in 2005, and Arsene Wenger, whose

Arsenal side reached the final a year later, enjoyed modest careers. Jose Mourinho, the manager of champion clubs in three countries, had no professional career at all.

Without question Mourinho is a master of the modern game. He owed his initial opportunity to Bobby Robson, then the manager of Sporting Lisbon, who needed an interpreter. Mourinho got the job, and followed his sponsor first to Porto, and then, in 1996, to Barcelona, where Robson won the European Cup-Winners Cup. After Robson's departure the Portuguese remained as assistant coach, and by 2002 he was back in his native land as manager of Porto.

His achievements in two years there were remarkable. Porto won the championship twice, the domestic cup, and two major European finals. Beating Celtic 3–2 in the Uefa Cup Final was a notable effort. Winning the Champions League in 2004, after thrashing Monaco 3–0, confirmed Mourinho as a man of his time, and Chelsea promptly emptied their piggy bank to turn their bunch of not-quiters into champions.

It took Mourinho all of a season to do that. Having done it, he did it again. He had then won four championships in successive years, and lived up to his own estimation as 'a special one'. His uneasy relationship with Roman Abramovich, the club's interfering owner, meant that his days at Stamford Bridge were likely to end at any time, and he left London in September 2007. Appointed manager of Internazionale of Milan in the summer of 2008 he immediately won another championship at the first attempt. It is an astonishing record.

And yet, and yet. There was something not entirely wholesome about Mourinho's time in England. Chelsea were immensely successful, sure, but they made little attempt to play with grace. For all the millions they spent on recruiting an international cast on the field, and another one on the bench, they were happy to grind out results in an efficient, often joyless manner. Given the players at their disposal they could have been so much more.

Nor was Mourinho's behaviour graceful. Calling himself 'a special one' was just about all right, for he was a winner who liked to present an impression of worldly detachment. But his refusal to acknowledge that Liverpool had beaten his team at Anfield, in a Champions League semi-final decided by a disputed goal, made him look small. When he threw a championship medal into the crowd at Stamford Bridge, after Chelsea had defended their prize in 2006, it was the act of an infant, not an adult marked down for special things.

There were comparisons with the young Clough, which Mourinho did nothing to deflect. The elder manager, who died in the autumn of Mourinho's first season at Chelsea, gave him an approving nod. But whereas the young Clough could be witty as well as abrasive, Mourinho's grandstanding was less agreeable. At times it looked malicious.

Returning to Barcelona in March 2005, for a Champions League quarter-final tie, Mourinho accused Anders Frisk, the Swedish referee, of meeting Frank Rijkaard, the Barcelona manager, at half-time. It was a false accusation, as he was forced to concede, but the damage had been done. Frisk, who subsequently received death threats, retired from the game, and, in a notable phrase, Volker Roth of Uefa called the Chelsea manager 'the enemy of football'.

In October 2006 Mourinho was at it again, accusing the Reading club of acting tardily when Petr Cech, the Chelsea goalkeeper, was involved in a collision that left him with a fractured skull. Reading responded with a point-by-point rebuttal of the accusations, exposing Mourinho's outburst as bluster. It was another example of the showman in him trying to undermine the professional reputations of people, in this case the team of paramedics, who had acted without fault.

Being a successful manager was never enough for Mourinho. He had also to play to the gallery. On occasions it was fun. Putting his finger to his lips, to silence Liverpool supporters at the League Cup Final of 2005, after Chelsea had equalised, was a playful gesture. Calling Arsene Wenger 'a voyeur' was less amusing, and in time even Mourinho was forced to admit he had overstepped the mark.

What did for him was the constant need to show off. The gnomic utterances, the finely calibrated displays of mock anger and mock puzzlement, designed to keep himself at the centre of attention, ensured that he put himself before his players, which is no place for a manager. Perhaps this was the frustrated performer in him, the self-styled 'turn' who sought different ways to entertain the audience he had cultivated so assiduously. For a while it was diverting. Presently it became tiresome. People who imagine themselves to be 'characters', who like to subvert the expectations they have taken such trouble to raise, usually are pretty tiresome.

In *The Old Country*, his play about treachery and belonging, Alan Bennett asks: 'It's all very well never to do what is expected of you, but what do you do when the unexpected is what people have come to expect?'

What indeed?

33 Graham Poll

Nobody looked more like a referee than Jack Taylor. The Wolverhampton butcher embodied the English yeoman: rugged, honest, dependable. His type saw service at Agincourt and Rorke's Drift. Given the honour of refereeing the World Cup Final of 1974 between West Germany and Holland, he walked on to the Munich pitch with the ball in his mighty right mitt, as if to say: 'I'm in charge here.'

The final was a minute old when Uli Hoeness fouled Johan Cruyff, and Taylor pointed to the penalty spot, from which Johan Neeskens put Holland ahead. Later he gave the Germans a penalty, from which Paul Breitner brought the scores level. Taylor was unbiddable, a man without fear or favour.

There were others at the time nearly as good. Clive Thomas could never be accused of being shy, but was good. Gordon Hill, liked by players for sharing the occasional crack, was highly regarded. Pat Partridge was another reliable decision-maker. There were some martinets, because a uniform tends to attract show-offs, and officialdom has been known to exalt the little chap, but English football was run by some pretty good men.

It still is, by and large. Unless he has a clear idea of duty, a fit constitution, and a will of iron, why would a man willingly endure the abuse of truculent players, the reflexive scorn of disappointed managers, and the hostility of crowds whose definition of a good decision is one that enables their team to win?

Unlike players, who contest the clearest decisions out of a misguided loyalty to the team, and then moan like mad when their appeals are overlooked, referees are at least familiar with the laws of the game. In order to reach the top levels they must slog through the foothills of the amateur leagues, so even the least impressive of them have demonstrated a love of football that is not always apparent in the highly paid whingers who undermine their authority.

It follows that the best referees are men of some character, and Graham Poll was one of the best of his time. He made mistakes, as they all do. In a World Cup match between Croatia and Australia in 2006 he gave Josip Simunic two yellow cards, and permitted the offender to remain on the field before a third did for him. So Poll missed out on the chance of taking the final, as Taylor had done.

Sheffield United supporters will need no reminding of Freddie Ljungberg's winner for Arsenal in an FA Cup semi-final at Old Trafford in 2003. The chance came after Michael Tonge, a Sheffield midfield player, collided with Poll, who allowed play to continue. Arsenal won the final, so it is fair to say that Poll is not the most popular man in the city of steel.

In retirement his stock has fallen. In fact he has become a

bit of a bore. On radio, on television and in print, Poll has been elevated to Grand Inquisitor status. At times it seems that errant officials may be invited to visit his chamber to recant their sins of omission and commission, or face his vengeance. It might be interesting to seek a referee's judgment on occasions. To see Poll sitting in permanent session in his judicial robes is not particularly illuminating. His ubiquity makes him look like a media tart.

Poll's willingness to provide 'good copy' has ensured that he will be remembered not for a decision he made, but one he ducked. He should have sent off Wayne Rooney, he is now happy to reveal, but chose not to. Rooney, playing for Manchester United, swore at him twenty-seven times in the most explicit way, yet Poll, eager to extend one more chance to the foul-mouthed striker, allowed him to stay on the field.

'There was an expectancy', he has written (meaning expectation), 'to manage a game with tolerance, understanding and empathy.' Dear oh dear. This is the canting drivel of a social worker.

Given an unmissable chance to uphold the law, Poll opted to pardon a man who was virtually begging to be dismissed. A referee like Taylor would have dispatched Rooney, no questions asked. One may conclude that Poll indulged him because he was a star. Would he have been so lenient with a less well-known offender? Hardly. The modern official likes to be pally with the big names.

Had he supplied a red card, everybody would have benefited. Rooney would have had the chance to reflect on his folly, and players up and down the country would have learned a valuable lesson: abuse the ref once, and you're off. In a game where raw emotion is valued above all else there is no more important lesson to learn. Yet, with the goal of public opinion at his mercy, Poll hoofed the ball into the stands.

So when he judges referees for not applying the law, we are entitled to draw attention to that ricket, and wonder whether, for all his knowledge of the laws, he has not done more to undermine the status of his colleagues than any number of red-faced managers and brattish players. This is not *High Noon*, Mr Poll, and you are not Gary Cooper. It's time to return your badge.

34 Sir Alf Ramsey

English football owes Sir Alf Ramsey a debt of honour. Upon his appointment as manager of the national team in 1962 he assured the public that his players would win the World Cup four years later, when England staged the tournament. People were sceptical. He had taken Ipswich Town to the championship that year but was that adequate preparation for jousting with the strongest sides in the world?

As we know, Ramsey proved the doubters wrong. The promotion of Bobby Moore to captain at the age of twenty-two was a masterstroke. So was the shifting of Bobby Charlton from the left wing to the marauding role in central midfield where he was to become a world-beater. In the year leading up to the team's supreme triumph he was not afraid to ditch experienced players, and introduce the likes of Nobby Stiles, Alan Ball, Geoff Hurst, Martin Peters and even Jack Charlton, a combative but limited centre half, who all contributed significantly to the eventual success.

The man who contributed most in the final, Geoff Hurst, remains the only man to have scored a hat-trick in a World Cup Final. He made the team because Ramsey was prepared

to drop Jimmy Greaves, the greatest goalscorer England has ever known. The photographer who caught Greaves on the final whistle, reflecting on what might have been, snapped one of the sport's saddest images. But the manager had made good his vow. England, by no means the most talented team in the competition, ended it as world champions.

Four years later they had an even better side. Everybody looked forward to a final between England and Brazil, who had contested a classic match in the qualifying group, won 1–0 by the Brazilians. That was the match of Gordon Banks's save from Pelé's header, and Moore's tackle on Jairzinho. But it was not to be. Banks, a victim of food poisoning, was forced to sit out the quarter-final with West Germany, and a two-goal lead evaporated after his replacement, Peter Bonetti, waved through a stoppable shot from Franz Beckenbauer.

Ramsey was blamed after that defeat for withdrawing Charlton from the field, with England two goals in front, to save him for the semi-final. In fact there was some merit in the manager's thinking. Charlton was thirty-two, tiring in the savage heat, and the man who replaced him, Colin Bell, was a magnificent athlete. But it was considered a blunder as Uwe Seeler equalised with a freakish header and then Gerd Muller, 'Der Bomber', volleyed the winner.

The defeat proved to be the prelude to a disappointing last act as England manager. When England next met the Germans, at Wembley twenty months later, for a place in the semi-final of the European Championship, the teams were less evenly matched. That was the night Gunter Netzer, the brilliant Borussia

Moenchengladbach midfielder, virtually played England on his own. The 3–1 victory showed how much ground Ramsey's team had ceded to opponents who had begun to embrace the Dutch notion of 'total football'.

For the return leg in Berlin Ramsey packed his team with defenders. Peter Storey, the Arsenal defender, who should never have been let anywhere near an England team, was selected alongside Norman Hunter, Emlyn Hughes, Roy McFarland and Paul Madeley, and England duly secured a goalless draw. Afterwards Netzer joked that every England player had autographed his leg. England lost dignity that day, and it was Ramsey's doing.

Total football, a fancy foreign term for something he didn't understand, was beyond him. Ramsey was a meat-and-two-veg Englishman, and there is a time and a place for basic fare. There is no virtue in bending the knee to foreigners simply because they are foreign. In this case, though, English suspicion of the exotic was pure ignorance. The Dutch, led by the great Johan Cruyff, were changing football before everybody's eyes, and only the English affected not to notice. The sadness is that, with the likes of Bell, Colin Todd and the young Trevor Francis, they had players who might have adapted rather well. What 'total football' really meant was a dissolution of hard distinctions between defending and attacking.

Ramsey preferred limited football. In 1973 Poland beat England in Katowice. In October, they came to Wembley for the return fixture, needing a draw to qualify for the World Cup ahead of England. They got it, thanks to a goal from Domarski and an inspired display by Tomaszewski, their goalie, who had the game of his life. It was no fluke. Poland were good value for their third place at the World Cup.

Ramsey's twelve-year reign as manager had ended by then, and though he was entitled to feel bitter about the manner of his sacking, it seemed inevitable to everybody else. The world-beating manager had not moved with the times; nor had England. The beauty of Holland's football in the 1974 tournament showed the world just how football could be played, though it was Beckenbauer's Germans who carried off the prize in Munich, with Muller, the home-town hero, scoring the winner.

When England failed to qualify for the World Cup in 1978 they dropped out of the game's top stream, and have never regained their place. Ramsey cannot be held entirely responsible for that. But the rot set in on his watch, when he sent out cloggers like Storey to silence ball-players like Netzer. They were grim days.

35 Antonio Rattin

The most poisonous fixture in international sport is a football match between England and Argentina. Wherever the location, whatever the context, the fur will fly.

In 1977 Trevor Cherry and Daniel Bertoni were sent off in Buenos Aires after the England defender's robust tackle brought a punch in response – and that was a so-called friendly. Nine years later, in an act of bare-faced larceny, Diego Maradona fisted an infamous goal in a World Cup quarter-final, and then attributed it to 'the hand of God'.

In 1998 David Beckham was dismissed in another World Cup quarter-final, after catching Diego Simone with an unnecessary flick of his leg. Simone, naturally, went down as though he had been speared by a harpoon, and England lost a match of two disputed spot-kicks on penalties. Afterwards the Argentinian players made insulting gestures to the England party as they left the ground in their coach.

England, unlucky to lose that night, were fortunate to win the next World Cup meeting between the sides, in Japan, four years later, when Beckham scored from yet another disputed penalty. If the English despise Maradona,

it is fair to say the Argentinians do not speak highly of Michael Owen.

There is always a whiff of cordite in the air when these players, from contrasting football cultures, meet. Yet, though they come from worlds of entirely different perceptions, the English were responsible for the game taking root in Argentina. The fact that the country's leading clubs, River Plate and Boca Juniors, have English names bears testimony to that inheritance. By tradition the Argentinians look up to England as the motherland of football, which accounts in part for the bitterness that clings to the fixture like ivy.

The most infamous act of all came in the first of those World Cup quarter-final meetings, at Wembley, in 1966. Having emerged with no great style from their qualifying group, England were confronted by an able team captained by Antonio Rattin, whose idea of leadership when a free kick went against him was to argue so vehemently that the German referee, Rudolph Kreitlein, sent him off for 'violence of the tongue' (even though Kreitlein understood no Spanish). It was only ten minutes later, after Rattin had staged a sit-down protest on the royal carpet, that he eventually left the action, to resounding jeers. Even then he wiped his hands on a corner flag bearing the royal ensign as he headed for the tunnel.

Sir Alf Ramsey, watching appalled from the dug-out, instructed his players not to exchange shirts afterwards with their opponents, and then raised the temperature a few degrees by calling the Argentinians 'animals'. Ever since, the teams have stepped on to the field together as if looking for landmines, and they have never been disappointed. Ramsey must share some responsibility for what has happened in the decades since that game, but Rattin's is the lion's share. Not even the magnificent performances of Osvaldo Ardiles during a distinguished career at Tottenham have improved relations between the countries.

Obviously the Falklands War of 1982, four years after Ardiles joined Tottenham with his compatriot, Riccardo Villa, did nothing to improve the situation. Indeed, Maradona, a superb footballer but a grubby human being, tried to justify his punched 'goal' in 1986 by claiming that it amounted to revenge for his country's military defeat. To rob a thief is to earn a thousand pardons, and all that gubbins. Such people should have no support but Maradona is regarded as a national hero. For once Brecht was right: unhappy is the land that needs heroes.

In the autumn of his years Rattin became a politician in the post-Falklands Argentina, and has expressed feelings of regret for his part in the Wembley disgrace. He even instructed his daughters to learn English and German, to try to avoid the kind of language difficulties that he had that sorry day with Kreitlein. But his bequest is poisonous. He did more than anybody to take a sporting fixture into a world where diplomatic correspondents would feel quite at home. He cannot be held accountable for all the things that have happened since that unpleasant day at Wembley, but he lit a fuse that still burns.

Will the twain ever meet? Fat chance. Despite the famous remark of Jorge Luis Borges that the Falklands War was a case of 'two bald men fighting over a comb', history has a habit of intruding. For many Argentinians it will always be a badge of honour to beat the English, by any means necessary. Some years ago, at a function to welcome members of MCC, one of the locals, who had returned to run the family estate in Argentina after his schooling in England, struck up a conversation with a touring cricketer.

'You shouldn't think', he said, 'that cricket is the main sport in this country', as if the tourists harboured any doubt. 'Football's the thing here, and the big game of the year is River Plate against Boca Juniors.'

'Really?' asked the guest, looking across the room for signs of intelligent life.

'Yes', the local said. 'There's nothing like it in England.'

'Is that so?'

'No, nothing. Except perhaps Eton against Harrow.'

Two cultures. One very wobbly bridge.

36 Charles Reep

After hearing *The Marriage of Figaro* Emperor Joseph II of Austria informed Mozart there were 'a great many notes in your score'. The composer replied: 'Not a note too many.' In a way it's reassuring to know that, even in the Age of Reason, the intellectual movement in which Joseph showed such interest, there were so many dunderheads.

Joseph was a man of his time. The Habsburg court really did rate other Viennese composers above Mozart, who, lest we forget, died in poverty. Just as the Football Association really did think Charles Hughes was the man to supervise the nation's coaches. His grumble was not too many notes. It was too many passes.

Hughes, appointed the FA's director of coaching in 1990, had learned at the foot of Wing Commander Charles Reep, an accountant by training, who scrutinised footballers as though he was counting pennies. Taken together, the Wing Co and the man who amplified his views were responsible for the damaging view that passing was strictly for pansies and foreigners.

Watching football in the 1950s, Reep took to writing up his opinions in the magazine *Match Analysis*. This man of figures proved to his satisfaction that 85 per cent of goals came from moves of fewer than three passes, so the ball should be moved up the field as swiftly as possible. It is Reep we have to thank for the phrase, 'position of maximum opportunity', or POMO as it came to be known.

Out of POMO came 'the long ball', which footballers have used for as long as the game has been played. Like everything else the direct method has its place. Reep wanted that place to be at the heart of every game. An article he published in 1962, called 'Are We Getting Too Clever?', summarised a view that said: do only what is absolutely necessary. Since then far too many English coaches have been happy to take him at his word.

Civilisation may be described as the sum of all those things that are not essential. In sport, too, the joy comes from flourishes that owe nothing to a grand design. That smells too much of that much-quoted prop, the 'drawing board', which has done so much to squeeze the fun out of life. There are no drawing boards in sport. There are only players, equipped with different skills, whose actions are determined by the situations in which they find themselves.

This was not a view that commended itself to Reep. In 1983, thirty years after Hungary had walked all over England at Wembley, winning 6–3 in a game that made their reputation, the master theorist would still not back down. In another essay, 'The Great Magyar Myth Exploded', he supplied facts and figures to suggest that Ferenc Puskas and his merry band had followed his methods to the letter.

England conquered the world in 1966. Since then they haven't come close. For many players, equipped from an early age with 'big engines', a sure touch of the ball is the last thing they acquire. What, foreigners like to joke, do you call an English player's second touch? A sliding tackle. To this day there is a suspicion among those who nurture young players that physical strength can compensate for lack of skill. Strength is indeed a winning quality but it should only support what is already there. It will never by itself transplant the skills of ball retention.

How many careers were ruined by the antediluvian attitudes of Reep and his followers? Dozens. Had Glenn Hoddle been born in continental Europe he would never have been left out of a national side. In England he was damned as a 'luxury' player; a Fortnum and Mason midfielder. What nonsense. Gifted players, those who 'invent' the game, as the Italians say, are essential. Without people who can master the ball there is little point in taking the field.

Thankfully, the pansies and foreigners paid little attention to Reep, for which we must thank our lucky stars. When Brazil won the World Cup in 1970 with a team of all the talents, they scored a goal of such distinction that it has gone down in football folklore as the finest of all time. It was a beautiful goal, not in the way that *Figaro* is a beautiful opera, but beautiful all the same. In movement and passing it was the most complete goal football has yet provided.

The scorer was Carlos Alberto, the captain, but only after every member of the side except Felix, the goalie, Everaldo and Piazza had been given a touch of the ball. Clodoaldo, Gerson,

Rivelino, Jairzinho and Tostão, great players all, were involved in the build-up, which began just outside the Brazil penalty area. When Pelé rolled the ball towards Alberto, who delivered his raking shot into the far corner of Dino Zoff's goal, it felt like a benediction. They had given the world a gift to remember them by.

Here was a goal for the ages. But why listen to the song of dazzling Brazilians when you can thump the ball downfield and give chase like Cherokees? As ye Reep, so shall ye sow.

37 Don Revie

Don Revie should be regarded as one of the towering figures of the English game. Instead, beyond a few parishes in Yorkshire, where keepers of the flame maintain a lonely vigil to defend a reputation that curdled long ago elsewhere, he is considered to be a deeply flawed man, who made his club's name mud and betrayed his country.

All human beings are flawed. What makes the great great is how they rise above their flaws so that, when their lives are weighed, the balance lies in their favour. In that respect Revie cannot be compared to his distinguished contemporaries because the team he built in his image at Elland Road, while it has never been forgotten, has rarely been forgiven. Whether Leeds fans like it, and it is clear that many do not, they must lump it. Revie's legacy is not a happy one.

For one wonderful year the brakes came off. Leeds began the 1973/4 campaign by winning eight successive matches, launching a season that ended in glory. Few English sides of any era could have lived with those champions, who so nearly added the European Cup a year later, under Jimmy Armfield, a very different man. Armfield smoked a pipe, played the organ at his church in Blackpool, and smiled easily. He wasn't likely to prosper at Leeds, and, after a decent start, he didn't. Revie, meanwhile, went to do the England job, where, with a frown forever on that careworn face, he was to write another ignoble chapter in his life's story.

Neutrals took against Leeds for perfectly sound reasons. They kicked like mules, and cheated like Sicilian bandits. Attempted bribery, sanctioned by the manager, was not beyond them. Then, like Claudius, they had the gall to smile: 'To smile, and smile, and be a villain!' Revie instructed them to greet the crowd with friendly gestures from the centre circle when they took the field, which, to be fair, took some gumption because the abuse returned by those crowds left the players in no doubt what people thought of them.

They were an unlovely bunch, yet it could have been so different. Given the abundance of talent at their disposal, they should have won so much more than they did. John Giles and Billy Bremner formed one of the great midfield partnerships. In Norman Hunter, Paul Reaney and Paul Madeley they had accomplished defenders. Allan Clarke was a natural goalscorer, and Eddie Gray would surely, had he been granted a career free of serious injuries, have developed into a world star. It was a formidable meshing of skills but the overall impression was one of sourness.

'I hope nobody ever tells them how good they are,' Brian Clough used to say when he was at Derby County. 'If they do, the rest of us won't win a thing.' Too often, though, Leeds were the bridesmaids. They finished runners-up five times under

Revie, winning the First Division only twice. They lost two FA Cup Finals, and a European Cup-Winners Cup Final. Many of their fans thought they were the victims of a conspiracy, that too many important decisions went against them. Others felt there was a poetic justice in their disappointments, particularly when a court heard how they had tried to bribe Wolves players at Molineux in the final fixture of the 1972 season. Wolves won 2–1, to deny Leeds the 'double' of League and FA Cup. The champions were Derby, fashioned by Clough along entirely different lines.

The most painful blow came in Paris the year after Revie's departure, when they lost 2–0 to Bayern Munich in the European Cup Final. Peter Lorimer, another of their former manager's stalwarts, had what appeared to be a good goal scrubbed for offside. Life at Elland Road was never the same after that, and the club gradually fell into desuetude despite the best efforts of former players such as Bremner, Clarke and Gray to revive their fortunes.

For all his experience as a club manager, Revie could never forge an alliance with the England players, though his period in office began deceptively well. There was even a rare victory over the Germans, in March 1975, when Revie gave Alan Hudson, the Stoke City midfielder, his first cap. He won only one more. He still won one cap more than Charlie George, who was playing the best football of his life at Derby County. He was withdrawn after an hour against the Republic of Ireland, when Revie plonked him on the left wing. Denied day-to-day involvement with players, in a club environment where he felt comfortable, with strong men like Giles and Bremner to provide a buttress, he was lost.

Obsessed by dossiers on opponents, which the players only pretended to read, Revie turned in on himself. The man who had been such an enterprising striker in his own playing days, a deep-lying centre forward of some craft, set his face against high skill when he had the best opportunity to choose it. For his last home match in charge of England, against Scotland at Wembley in May 1977, he selected a leaden-footed midfield of Brian Talbot, Brian Greenhoff and Ray Kennedy. Scotland won 2–1. The manner of defeat amounted to an abdication and within a month Revie had done a bunk, to the United Arab Emirates, where the money was better and the pressure less intense. People regretted the manner of his departure, not the fact that he had gone.

It was a grubby ending, and nobody let him forget it. His former players stood by him, for they had seen the more generous side of his complex character, and had much to be grateful for. The rest of the world saw only an unhappy, disloyal man who, when he could have done so much for the game, opted to befoul and then betray it.

38 Peter Ridsdale

Dreams, as Dr Freud taught us, disconcert more often than soothe. In our sleeping hours we rarely see fluffy lambs gambolling across a verdant meadow, or hear birds tweeting in blue skies. We are more likely to count numbers that go on for ever, or fall from mighty heights with nothing to cushion the landing.

So maybe Peter Ridsdale was thinking of the Viennese physician when he spoke, on stepping down as chairman of Leeds United in March 2003, with the club close to breaking-point, of 'living the dream'. In their case the numbers did go on for ever, and the club had fallen so far from grace that it cannot be said with certainty they have landed yet.

The debt had reached £103 million when Ridsdale packed his bags, and although they avoided relegation that spring, they went down a year later, and are now members of English football's third tier. As far as Leeds fans are concerned their erstwhile chairman's performance was not so much a dream as a nightmare from which they have yet to emerge.

Others shared the blame, notably David O'Leary, a manager promoted above his station, who proceeded to spend money

like a drunken sailor on shore leave. It was O'Leary who handed
over £7 million to Derby County for the services of a bog-
standard midfield player called Seth Johnson. Oh yes, they
lived the dream all right.

O'Leary was merely a rating. Ridsdale wore the captain's
pips, and it was his *grand projet* that scuppered the ship.
Intoxicated by the team's success in 2001, when they reached
the semi-finals of the Champions League, he borrowed £60
million, against projected future income based on involvement
in European competition, only to see the vessel go down within
a year.

Dismissed in the summer of 2002, O'Leary gave way to Terry
Venables, star of television studio, Scribes West nightclub and
the High Court, who lasted all of nine months. That really was
a clever appointment. Never two without three, they say, and
along came Peter Reid, who had just been relieved of his
managerial duties by Sunderland. It was Ridsdale's final act as
chairman.

Yorkshire folk with gallows humour recalled Viv Nicholson,
the pools winner from Castleford, who vowed to 'spend, spend,
spend!' Ridsdale, desperate to join the rich men at football's
top table, had done it with other people's money. In that glory
year, 2001, when the sky seemed the limit, he paid himself
£645,000.

The best players left, so that Leeds could pay their bills. Rio
Ferdinand, bought two years before from West Ham United, was
moved on to Manchester United in 2002 for £29 million. He was
followed out of Elland Road by Jonathan Woodgate, Robbie Keane

and anybody else who commanded a decent fee. Relegation came in 2004. A year later Ken Bates marched into town as chairman. Within two seasons they had been relegated again.

Ridsdale was a long way down the road by then. In September 2003, five months after leaving Leeds, the dreamer of dreams had taken over at Barnsley, where he spent fifteen months. Undeterred by his failure to make much of a mark there he joined Cardiff City, first as vice-chairman, before he succeeded Sam Hammam as chairman of the Welsh club.

The lifelong Leeds fan had not forgotten his first love. In 2007 Ridsdale published *United We Fall*, an attempt to put the record straight, or at least supply an alternative account of his time as helmsman. It was not considered a mighty success. People still thought of its author as the man who kept a goldfish in the boardroom.

Ridsdale's own journey was far from over. In June 2009 his consultancy firm, WH Sports Group Ltd, went into liquidation with debts of £410,000. The question that struck observers was simple: who would approach a man whose chequered career in football administration was a matter of public record for advice about anything?

His dreams of glory had brought only heartache. The club he supported, and tried so hard to transform into champions of England and then Europe, had become a byword for incompetence on and off the field. Casting his net wider, beyond Yorkshire, he found further disappointment.

There are many rogues in football. Peter Ridsdale is not one of them. Like many an ambitious football-loving businessman before him, who saw reputations to be made, he claimed to have a vision which ultimately turned out to be a mirage. Now that he is older and wiser, would he have done anything differently? Probably not.

39 Robinho

It took a long time for English football to come to terms with foreigners. Bert Trautmann, the German whose talents in goal were recognised in a St Helens prisoner-of-war camp, and who later joined Manchester City, was for years an exception to the rule written in jest by Flanders and Swann: 'The English, the English, the English are best. I wouldn't give tuppence for all of the rest.'

Even after Trautmann had made his mark, playing on through a broken neck to win an FA Cup winner's medal in 1956 and earn his place in the annals, some people needed to be persuaded that those unfortunates who had grown up on the other side of the channel could play a bit. When Hungary came to Wembley in 1953, an English observer took a look at the portly Ferenc Puskas, and said: 'We'll piss it.' Six goals later, the world looked slightly different. Puskas, the ringmaster, cracked his whip again the following year, in Budapest, and England shipped seven more goals. Palpably the English were not the best. They never had been.

From this vantage-point, when every Premier League side is awash with foreign talent, and even the lower league clubs

have acquired a few of their own, that post-war world seems as remote as the Hanoverians. The reliance on overseas talent has changed the nature of our national game, for better, for worse. The quid is that the best players have dignified the game, and helped to bring on English youngsters; the quo that England are not grooming enough players of their own.

Many imports have performed superbly. Eric Cantona, Denis Bergkamp and Gianfranco Zola did more to transform the fortunes of their clubs than any native-born players, and there are dozens more who have played their part. In terms of value for money the Norwegians have been particularly good, with the Serbs and Croats not far behind. The Dutch, from the days of Arnold Muhren and Franz Thijssen at Ipswich, have excelled in England, as they generally do wherever they go.

So Robinho, the Brazilian striker, had a lot to live up to when he joined Manchester City in the autumn of 2008. He had been all set to go to Chelsea before a change of ownership enabled City to offer Real Madrid £32 million for his twinkling boots. Madrid, who had become fed up with the player's reluctance to make the most of his talents, were happy to accept the money.

For twenty minutes it all went well. Robinho scored midway through the first half of his debut – against Chelsea – and the fans imagined they had found a new hero, even after Chelsea, stung by the insult, ran out convincing winners. Then things turned sour. It became clear that, for all his gifts, Robinho was a lazy player, who considered the other members of the team to be below the salt. His peculiar gesture on scoring a goal, sticking his thumb in his mouth, was a damning form of revelation. Here was a big baby.

Week by week the evidence mounted. He cut a training camp in Tenerife to fly back to Brazil, without the club's permission. He turned up at Manchester airport for a trip to Europe with his shirt hanging out, wearing white pumps. This was not just a thoughtless act in defiance of the club's dress code. It seemed to tell the world, in a manner that brooked no argument: I am a clown.

There were allegations that he had sexually assaulted a girl in a Leeds nightclub. Although Robinho denied the allegation and no charges were brought, the question lingered: what was a Manchester-based Brazilian doing in a club in Yorkshire? Nor did it help his reputation that Pelé, speaking unguardedly to reporters back in Brazil, referred to Robinho's alleged use of narcotics. Robinho dismissed the allegation as 'absurd'. Pelé withdrew his claim, but people were beginning to form a less than flattering picture of a man paid £160,000 a week to play football for a living.

Nothing embarrassed him quite so much, however, as his performances in a City shirt. The man brought in to raise the profile of the club was invisible for large chunks of matches, going three months without scoring, and eventually being dropped by Hughes. When Roberto Mancini succeeded Hughes he too found Robinho's charms resistable. The Brazilian scored one goal, against mighty Scunthorpe in the FA cup, and was shipped out on loan to Santos. It was a humiliation for player and club.

Ah, said some in his defence, but he's a Brazilian. They do things differently there. They like to 'have a good time' when they're not playing. Cut the chap a bit of slack. And then one thought of Juninho, the Brazilian midfielder, who won the respect of the Middlesbrough supporters for his wholehearted performances, week in, week out. If you go to another land to play football, particularly if the move makes you very rich, the least you can do is absorb the professional practices of your peers. Robinho, who never really understood which club he was joining, was not interested in such trifles. He was a Brazilian international, and that was enough.

Manchester City have been blessed by the exceptional service of the foreigner who made the greatest contribution to the English game. They have also endured the excesses of a thumb-sucker who couldn't wait to go home. Mercenary is an ugly word in any tongue. Where Robinho is concerned the rebuke is richly deserved.

40 Cristiano Ronaldo

When Cristiano Ronaldo left Old Trafford in June 2009, it was to the sound of one hand clapping. He had finally got the move he wanted, to Real Madrid, and nobody shed a tear at his passing. Even Manchester United fans had their doubts about the man. Beyond Manchester there was no doubt: he was a preening prat, a puffed-up popinjay, a pouting prancer, who happened to be a good footballer.

Ronaldo is a bit better than that. In his six years in England the Portuguese became a very good player, not that far off a great one, who made and scored goals – forty-two in one extraordinary season. But he also acquired a reputation as the most devout worshipper at the shrine of Thespis, and a colossal whinger. He made his professional life here, but he never chose to fit in, so people were quite untouched by his departure.

In his final season at Old Trafford, when United won their third Premier League on the trot, claimed the World Club Championship and reached the Champions League Final, Ronaldo was so detached from his team-mates and the supporters that he seemed to live on an island of his own. Most foreign players are accepted. Some come to be loved. Ronaldo

of the dazzling heels and thunderbolt shot was only ever respected as a player, and then through gritted teeth.

His flirtation with Madrid was only part of his relentless need to be at the centre of attention. For this young man (he was only twenty-four when he joined Real) is a narcissist for all seasons. In his final weeks with United his behaviour became intolerable, as he moaned all afternoon during a defeat at Fulham and then publicly challenged Sir Alex Ferguson's decision to withdraw him for his own good in the second half of the Manchester derby, when United were beating City comfortably.

This urge to show off was part of a pattern. When United won the Champions League Final in Moscow in 2008, beating Chelsea on penalties, Ronaldo did not at first join his team-mates as they celebrated their victory. He remained on the halfway line, weeping conspicuous tears of relief and joy in such a manner that the television cameras could not fail to pick him out. He had just missed a penalty, by trying to be clever, so he imagined the story was about him.

There are many things wrong with English football, but the notion of team spirit shows our game at its best. It doesn't mean that non-conformists cannot belong. It means that, while their skills may be admired, they should never put themselves above the game. The pouting Portuguese did it so frequently that you could almost set your clock by it.

The worst example came in Gelsenkirchen when England met Portugal for a place in the semi-finals of the 2006 World Cup. There could be no doubt about the Argentinian referee's decision to dismiss Wayne Rooney for stamping on Ricardo

Carvalho but Ronaldo's hollering insistence that his United team-mate should walk, and then his knowing wink to the team bench once Rooney had been sent off, revealed something deeply unpleasant.

That is the impression that will linger longest in many English minds. Not the brilliant teenager who joined United from Sporting Lisbon for £12 million, and elevated himself to the pantheon of Old Trafford stars. Not the man who scored spectacular goals from thirty or even – as against Benfica – forty yards, and who could be mentioned in the same breath as George Best without embarrassment. Not the man who won the Ballon d'Or and the Fifa World Player of the Year award for his brilliant performances in 2007/8.

No, Ronaldo the scheming little brat is the one who springs to mind. The one who did all those silly step-overs, to gild the lily. The one who crashed his Ferrari, on his second day behind the wheel, in a tunnel near Ringway airport. The one who barged into a meeting to mark the fiftieth anniversary of the Munich air disaster, and noisily interrupted Wayne Rooney, who was speaking, as he got fed up of waiting for him to finish. The one who flounced, and dived, and squawked, and winked, and spent two years agitating for the move of his dreams to Madrid.

When he got there, with a price of £80 million on his head, he did not disappoint. He told reporters that he was worth even more than the transfer fee the clubs had agreed. His former team-mates in Manchester would not have been surprised to learn of his estimation. 'It's all about him,' they complained after the Champions League Final against Barcelona, which the Spaniards won with a display of beautiful football.

That night in Rome United saw Ronaldo at his best for the first ten minutes. After that spirited burst, in which his detachment from the other ten players could not have been more clear, he was obliged to spend the rest of the evening admiring what properly committed team players can achieve. It was a masterclass of football as a team game.

Ronaldo achieved remarkable things at Old Trafford. But he will never be recalled with the love that Best still inspires, or the affection that 'Eric' can take for granted. He passed through Manchester almost reluctantly, leaving plenty of memories but no lasting mark. He came, he dazzled, he departed. Those who follow will look in vain for his footprints. They have vanished with the snows of yesteryear.

41 Richard Scudamore

Richard Scudamore, chief executive of the Premier League since 1999, would slip easily into Yum Yum's role in *The Mikado*. Put him in a frock, apply some make-up, push him towards the centre of the stage, and he could sing her song of hope very nicely. 'I mean to rule the earth as he the sky. We really know our worth, the sun and I.'

World domination is what Scudamore is after, and he will not cease from mental fight till he has built Jerusalem in every green and pleasant land beyond his own. This policy of *lebensraum* propelled his idea to introduce a thirty-ninth game in the Premier League fixture list, to be played in cities outside England, and one can almost hear him talking up its attractions. The prospect of watching some of the league's lesser lights going hammer and tongs should have the good folk of Kuala Lumpur racing to the ground to bag the best seats. Who wouldn't part willingly with $100 to watch Kevin Davies or Emile Heskey slice a sitter into the crowd? Roll up, roll up!

Sepp Blatter, the president of Fifa, the international game's ruling body, downed Scudamore's bird like a grouse-shooter on the Glorious Twelfth. 'An abuse of Association Football', he called it. But Scudamore will not be easily deflected. He knows the commercial power of the Premier League, which has not been tempered during his period in office. In 2007 he signed a television deal including worldwide rights worth £2.7 billion, so he may feel the future lies with him, not Blatter.

The plan was to introduce Premier League fixtures to five overseas cities from 2011, to establish 'new markets', or whatever the PR men like to say. So English football could, in the next decade, become a game played in part by English teams in the Far East and North America in order to satisfy sponsors. It is sport as brand recognition, which has more to do with flogging shirts than upholding the traditions of what Blatter called, quite properly, Association Football.

One hopes that Scudamore fails, for it cannot be right for the Premier League to trample into foreign lands like a conquering army. Nor is it easy to see how English clubs could fit a thirty-ninth game into their schedules when many of them are stretched to bursting point as it is. If Aston Villa and Bolton Wanderers could not be bothered to field full-strength sides in Uefa Cup knock-out fixtures when they were well placed to make progress, they will not find it easy to fulfil an additional fixture 5,000 miles away. As for the more successful clubs, who are involved in European club competitions more regularly, a thirty-ninth game is the last thing they need.

Far from putting a few eggs into foreign baskets Scudamore would do well to keep a tighter rein on events happening under his nose. For, while he was drawing up his plans to dazzle foreign audiences, a tale was unfolding in London that did his reputation no good.

The Carlos Tevez affair has become a *cause célèbre* for good reasons. In 2007 West Ham stayed up largely because the Argentinian striker scored a series of important goals, including the winner in the last match of the season at Old Trafford. Taken in conjunction with events elsewhere it meant that Sheffield United were relegated, a demotion they refused to take lying down. Eventually, after sixteen months of legal wrangling, a Football Association inquiry chaired by Lord Griffiths found in their favour, and West Ham were instructed to pay the Yorkshire club £15 million compensation.

Their beef was easy to understand. Tevez and Javier Mascherano, another Argentinian international, were not owned by West Ham, but by a consortium headed by Kia Joorabchian, an Anglo-Iranian agent, who had offered them to the club the previous autumn. The Premier League had accepted this was the case in April 2007 when they fined West Ham £5.5 million for breaching rules regarding 'third party' ownership, but it took the FA's will to press for an official inquiry, at which West Ham were revealed to be fibbers. Their claims to own the Argentinian pair were shown to be false, yet they avoided a points deduction that would have sent them down. No wonder Sheffield were incensed by the handling of the case. They reckoned that relegation would cost them £45 million in television revenue, sponsorship and ticket sales.

Why did the Premier League not dock West Ham points instead of issuing a fairly useless fine? Answer came there none from Scudamore, bringing a response from Yorkshire that some clubs were more equal than others. It was not the Premier League's finest hour.

There were calls for Scudamore's head but, cushioned by all that money, he's not a man who is troubled by self-doubt. It's back to Yum Yum. 'Ah pray make no mistake, we are not shy. We're very wide awake, the moon and I.'

42 Bill Shankly

'Thank you,' Paul Simon muttered just loud enough for his purpose, as the audience cheered Art Garfunkel for singing 'Bridge Over Troubled Water', 'I wrote that song.' Bill Shankly could have been forgiven for saying something similar after he handed over his Liverpool team in the summer of 1974 to Bob Paisley, and then saw his assistant go on to win trophies galore in the next decade. 'Thank you, I built that club.'

He did, for Liverpool were in the Second Division when he went to Anfield in 1959. They were known as 'Liddell-pool', made up of Billy Liddell and ten others, a poor second not only to Manchester United, where Matt Busby was remaking English football, in the aftermath of the Munich air crash, but also to Everton. The Toffeemen underlined their status by winning the championship in 1963, a year before Shankly put his pole on the mountain-top. That was the turning of the Mersey tide. They hooked the FA Cup the following year, then the championship again in 1966, and though there were then six barren seasons Shankly ended his reign in glory, winning the championship and Uefa Cup in 1973, and adding the FA Cup in 1974.

It was in the next decade that Liverpool really cleaned up, as his successor, once his right-hand man, constructed a side that dominated Europe as well as England. They were more attractive under Paisley, who brought in Kenny Dalglish, Alan Hansen, Graeme Souness, Ian Rush and Mark Lawrenson. Shankly's teams enjoyed success but, with the exception of Peter Thompson's wing play and Ian St John's quicksilver instincts near goal, they rarely stirred neutrals. The arrival of Dalglish from Celtic in the summer of 1977, to replace the Hamburg-bound Kevin Keegan, was the best business conducted by the manager of any English club. Liverpool even made £60,000 on the deal.

To Paisley the glory; to Shankly the praise. Along with Busby and Stan Cullis, he is one of the great club-builders. More than the others, he also established a bond between the club and its parent city that still exists. For all their success, which has brought worldwide fame, Liverpool remain a provincial club, in the best sense. Manchester United are an international business. Liverpool, despite the recent Spanish influence, remain rooted in native soil. If, at times, that postcode-consciousness is a touch overcooked for outsiders, the locals do not repine.

So how did this outstanding manager foul up football? For one overwhelming reason. It was Shankly who said, in a television interview in 1981, that the game was 'more important' than life and death. Not just more important, but 'much more' important. Whether it was uttered in jest, as some have maintained, he never disowned it. Trotted out from time to time as an example of his lacerating wit (though it proves nothing of the sort), the easily impressed have used it to justify all kinds of unpleasant things in the years since, in the expectation that others will swell the laughter of recognition.

Filtered through the minds of a thousand dullards it is considered to be one of sport's defining phrases, along with 'winning isn't everything, it's the only thing', which is usually attributed to Red Sanders, an American football coach. The only thing it defines is that those who quote it are buffoons. It also invites people to look at Shankly's other quips with a more critical eye, and the eye does not always like what it sees. 'That's not your leg,' he told injured players who he thought were malingering, 'it belongs to Liverpool FC.' Not exactly a rib-tickler, is it?

Shankly the man was obviously warm-hearted. Shankly the 'character' has not worn as well as his admirers would have us believe. What sort of person imagines that a trip to watch Rochdale reserves is an appropriate way to mark a wedding anniversary? A man who puts football above all other things, that's who, and there are plenty of adjectives for such people, not all of the kind routinely rolled out to pay homage to 'Shanks'.

'Aggressive self-pity' was the phrase that Edward Pearce, the journalist, applied to Liverpool. These are deep waters, for the city has many attractions, and there is another Liverpool that people do not always see. It is to Shankly's credit that he gave his adopted home so much to be proud of at a time when Liverpool's main commercial function, as a port that looked outward to the world, found itself facing the wrong way. But it is an ambiguous bequest. Liverpool fans have been spoilt by being told too often they are a breed apart, and Shankly did nothing to dampen that sense of exceptionalism.

There is a more complex view of Liverpool. Terence Davies, who was born in the city, has done his best to present it in his films, notably the bracingly unsentimental memoir, *Of Time and the City*, which, commendably, has nothing to do with football. However, while his work has earned an international reputation, Liverpool remains ambivalent. Davies, who prefers Shostakovich to Shankly, evades easy categorisation.

Shankly was one of the great managers, who deserves his memorial at Anfield. He made the club great. He was also a bit of a ninny. Sport is not 'much more' important than life or death – as those Liverpool fans who lost loved ones at Hillsborough could have told him – nor can his remark be laughed away as a merry jape by 'good old Shanks'. Football should only ever be a pleasant diversion, even in Liverpool.

43 Bob Shennan

Nothing has changed so much in post-war England as the nature of speech. The modern English person communicates in a way that would be unintelligible to somebody born a century ago. It has nothing to do with fads, which come and go, nor has it to do with accent. Provided they are not put on, local accents can be engaging. The change has to do with colour, rhythm and clarity of speech.

Listening to Five Live, the national radio station established in 1995, can be absolute torture. Gathered under its banner is a small army of barbarians who delight in mashing the world's richest language. In the course of a single news summary you can hear enough glottal stops, elisions, false stresses, rising inflections and sundry imprecisions to last a lifetime. Nobody seems to know how to pronounce the simplest of words, or to care. The use of active verbs is strictly voluntary, vowels are swallowed like oysters and a search party to find the letter T was abandoned long ago.

Many presenters rejoice in grammatical abuse. Their neglect underlines something that the novelist, Anthony Burgess, said on a trip to England towards the end of his life. Burgess spent most of his adult years living in Italy and Monaco, though he never lost sight of the fact that he belonged to a great literary culture (in his opinion, the greatest). 'Only in England,' he said, 'is the perversion of language regarded as a victory for democracy.'

Five Live sees itself not perhaps as a democratic station, whatever that means, but certainly as a demotic one. It may have started with the best of intentions, and employed fine broadcasters like Brian Hayes, but before long it found its level as Radio Mate, Radio Bloke or Radio Half-Wit, depending on the angle of observation. The man responsible was Bob Shennan, a former head of sport at the BBC, who assumed responsibility for the station in 2000 and, before he left eight years later, did nothing to rein in the worst offenders. One hapless continuity announcer is still there, talking about the joys of 'down-*louds*' and 'digit-*uw*' radio.

Like many people who glide to top jobs in the media, Shennan attended a grammar school before going to one of our two oldest universities. Again, like many of those fortunate folk, he seems to enjoy slumming it. And when Five Live acquired exclusive radio rights to cover Premier League football, and the station was transformed into a pleasure-dome of fandom, Shennan was able to slum it with the best.

He was not responsible for the appearance of Danny Baker on the phone-in. That pearly king was already taking calls when Shennan arrived. But what a falling-off there was! How could anybody imagine that Charlie Whelan, Gordon Brown's bruiser, would make a broadcaster? Well, Shennan did, persuaded no doubt by Whelan's attachment to football, and to one club in particular. Tottenham Hotspur got a mention every time he parked his buttocks in the Five Live studio.

With the station wedded so completely to football, which led its sports bulletins morning, noon and night, it was considered meet and right for presenters to bang on about the team they followed. The most relentless rattle-waver was Susan Bookbinder, who wore a Manchester City replica shirt at work and mentioned the club almost every day. It was Bookbinder who bade farewell to Wayne Rooney, who had graced the station with a guest appearance, with a breezy 'Thanks, Roo'. That was the genuine voice of Radio Mate, the station Shennan refined, and for which he was eventually rewarded, after a brief spell away from the BBC, with the stewardship of Radio 2.

There is no doubt that the obsession with football has unbalanced the rest of the sports coverage. When one sport is granted top billing, irrespective of the significance of events elsewhere, the nature of that coverage must change, not obviously for the better. In time there became a Five Live way of doing things, to the extent that even *Test Match Special*, the supreme sports programme in British broadcasting, became vulnerable to the new, demotic approach.

Although nobody within the BBC sports department was bold enough to say so publicly, there was a mistrust of *TMS*, partly because it was presented by old-fashioned broadcasters, who had county (rather than town) voices; partly because it had a large, loyal audience that knew nothing of Five Live. Some of the people being trained to take over *TMS* are equipped neither by talent nor by basic knowledge of the game to take it forward, but they speak in a way that is considered acceptable to a less discriminating audience. That is the real achievement of Five Live: to make sure that one size fits all. Slowly, drip by drip, programmes change, and the poor listener feels left out.

If there is one voice that defines this horrible new world it belongs to a man called Spoony. A disc jockey by background, he can be relied upon to make a clown of himself every time he addresses the mic. Words tumble out like a geyser, without rhyme or reason, so it could be said he makes an ideal host of the wretched phone-in.

The man who gave house room to this oaf, who finds the English language an unfathomable mystery, was Bob Shennan, who once declared his mission was to make Five Live 'relevant'. Good, clear English, apparently, is irrelevant. Into the stocks with him!

44 Peter Swales

Peter Swales was a wrong 'un. One of life's most obvious corporals, he spent two decades trying to pass himself off as a captain. As chairman of Manchester City between 1973 and 1994, he sacked no fewer than eleven managers. Installed as chairman of the Football Association's international committee, after greasing his way up the slippery pole, he engineered the dismissal of Bobby Robson. Give a man a big job, goes the old saw, and he will show you how small he can be. Swales was a small man.

Having made a modest fortune by selling television sets and record players to the south Manchester gentry, Swales joined the City board in 1971, and was elected chairman two years later. Let it not be said he looked anything less than the part. During his twenty-one years at the helm of a vessel that was not always seaworthy (they were relegated twice during his chairmanship), he was virtually a caricature of the self-made provincial businessman who fancied his chance running a football club.

Some provincial chairmen did a lot of good. Bob Lord, the Burnley butcher, made plenty of enemies with his plain speaking but they loved him at Turf Moor, for good reason. The Clarets won a championship in 1960, and reached the FA Cup Final two years later. For years the Lancashire club punched above their weight. Swales, like Doug Ellis at Aston Villa, was less loved. With his Cuban heels, comb-over hairdo, and a Mancunian whine that dropped sweet nothings into the laps of grateful reporters, he became a figure of fun.

Mockery didn't bother him in the slightest. He welcomed it, inviting the cameras into Maine Road at the drop of one of his battered hats. In 1977 he waved through a crew from *Nationwide*, the BBC's early-evening magazine programme, who spent an entire season on location, showing viewers 'how things were done' at a major club. What they saw, usually, was a dapper little chappie turning the charm on and off like a switch to one of the electrical appliances he used to flog.

Three years later he endorsed a grim fly-on-the-wall documentary, towards the end of Malcolm Allison's ill-starred homecoming. How viewers roared as the cameras peeped inside the boardroom where directors took it in turns to kiss the chairman's ring. This was big-time football recast as *The King and I*: 'Yes, your majesty; no, your majesty; just how low should we go, your majesty?'

Meanwhile the king dreamed of new lands to conquer. Swales was fond of telling reporters that City were 'the last team from Manchester to win the championship – and the next'. It was a decent line because City, champions in 1968, had a strong side when he joined the board, and their rivals were in decline. Indeed it was a goal back-heeled by Denis Law, wearing a blue shirt, that sent United down to the Second Division in 1974. Although the Reds were promoted at once, and won the FA Cup in 1977, City finished second that year, one point behind Liverpool, and their future prospects looked promising. They had bought a handful of international players, and brought some good ones through their acclaimed youth system.

The City chairman owes his place in the hall of shame for his wanton destruction of this inheritance. Malcolm Allison, who returned to Maine Road in 1979, has usually taken the blame for the recruitment of players at inordinate cost but it was Swales, the keeper of the till, who endorsed each transfer when he could have said 'No'. So desperate was he to take on United that not a day went by without him thinking of some ruse to upset them, on or off the field.

Every battlefield is littered with bodies, and Swales's heaviest defeat came in September 1979, when he permitted Allison to buy Steve Daley, a modest midfielder, from Wolves for an eye-popping £1,473,500. Asked on live television what he would say to fans who thought that coach and chairman had taken leave of their senses, Swales replied: 'Come and see him play tomorrow.' The supporters turned up. City duly lost 1–0.

Coming weeks after the acquisition of Steve Mackenzie, a Crystal Palace reserve, for £275,000, and Mike Robinson, who had turned up few trees at Preston North End, for £750,000, Daley's arrival was of a piece. There was to be no title for City, except the honorary one bestowed upon them for being football's undisputed barmpots. It couldn't work for poor Daley, who was obliged to bear a burden that was intolerable. After eighteen months of underachievement, which included an FA Cup defeat at Halifax Town of the old Fourth Division, he was moved on to Seattle Sounders in the North American Soccer League for £300,000.

It remains the worst misjudgement of a player ever made by an English club. Allison, apparently, was happy to offer Wolves £400,000 for the player. Swales amended the fee, though he denied doing so. He denied doing a lot of things, did Swales. He had a nose longer than Pinocchio's. By endorsing the Daley transfer he did not just muck up his own club's finances by inflating the value of an average player, he distorted the market for all clubs.

Swales showed no contrition. He sacked Allison, and went through every conceivable kind of manager before he was unseated himself in 1994, a year after he had dismissed Peter Reid, who had just committed the appalling mistake of taking the club to fifth place in the newly established Premier League. In his time in office the club won one trophy: the League Cup, in 1976. It was a poor return for such grand schemes.

Swales passed away in 1996, three days before City were relegated, happy to finish their final game playing for a draw when they needed to win. In death, as in life, the grim comedy continued.

45 Gordon Taylor

Footballers do not, as a rule, enjoy the way they are portrayed by the media. Although many well-known players are happy to trouser tidy fees for putting their names to ghost-written columns, in which they reveal not very much, they neither like nor respect the people who report their activities.

In recent years the chasm between the writers and the written-about has reached Amazonian proportions. Gone are the days when players and journalists caroused together, or exchanged yarns over scones and tea. Whereas other sportsmen are generally on good terms with those who follow them, footballers regard scribes with suspicion. At best they consider them to be battening wretches; at worst, troublemakers.

There is a sliver of truth in that interpretation. Newspapers do construct stories out of events, and those stories, taken together, over a period of weeks, help to furnish a 'narrative'. But players and managers assist the reporters by blundering into traps that, with a bit more thought, could easily be avoided. And it is certainly not true to say that newspapers will print anything to paint the game black. Indeed, there is plenty of evidence to suggest the boot is often on the other foot.

One England international, spotted staggering round the forecourt of a garage, told police officers that 'the youth of today look up to people like me'. Another international, in his cups, casually handed a taxi driver £1,000, to drive him home from central London to Manchester. Other capped players have committed acts of wrong-doing or folly. Perhaps the most startling offender was the player, banged up overnight in a police cell, who could not write his own name.

Then there are those who have been publicly exposed. Kieron Dyer, for instance, the diamond-encrusted wastrel, who pranged a flash car on the Tyne bridge. Another time he left his earrings in the dressing-room at West Bromwich Albion, and asked Bobby Robson whether the coach could go back to the Hawthorns so that he could retrieve them. The Newcastle manager told him his fortune.

All this points to one thing: a lack of education. Not education as in Eton and Balliol. There are plenty of chaps who attended those institutions who have also behaved badly. Rather, education in the sense of becoming rounded human beings, and understanding the responsibility that comes with being a rich sportsman. In that sense young footballers have not been particularly well served by the body that represents them. The least popular guests on the long-standing BBC television programme, *A Question of Sport*, are footballers. Most fear 'a ribbing from the lads' if they appear too intelligent. It reveals a lot about the game.

Gordon Taylor, the chief executive of the Professional Footballers' Association, receives a seven-figure annual salary, so it is not only the top players who earn a handsome living from the game. Yet how often has anybody heard him criticise the offensive, occasionally criminal behaviour of his members? He has to tread carefully, it is true. His job is to offer advice on professional and personal matters to his members, not all of whom are big stars. But the wider football public would like to hear a clearer voice from time to time, with regard to the significant minority of players whose antics have defiled the game.

For all the talk of 'rights', and Taylor is entitled to defend them, footballers must also be aware of their duties. The PFA seems to have spent more time assisting troublemakers, in their various rehabilitation periods, than helping the victims of their trouble. Some people are simply not worth bothering with.

Why can so few footballers speak confidently in front of a microphone or camera? Even experienced players look cowed whenever they are solicited for an opinion on a subject more taxing than their own performance. Few players try to deflect questions with a touch of humour or self-mockery, except some of the foreigners, who, it should be pointed out, come from similar social backgrounds. With a bit of effort, and guidance, it can be done.

A footballer's deportment in public ought to be part of that educational process. When they are taken on as apprentices all players should be made aware, for their own sake, of the importance of addressing members of the media. If their careers develop the way they hope, they will have to get used to it, so why not make a start at sixteen? It's not as if they lack the time to apply their minds to other matters. The working week for most players amounts to about twenty hours. There must be more profitable ways of spending their free time than idling in snooker halls or playing video games.

There is an important job here for the PFA and their highly paid chief executive. Taylor and his team should be trying to improve the lives of their members, in the broadest sense, not just looking after their immediate prospects. If footballers are upset by the bad press they get, and the public perception that most of them are thickos, they have only themselves to blame.

Taylor could make a start by brushing up his native tongue. In a radio interview he spoke of the need 'to step up to the plate', an Americanism so revolting that it should come with a statutory fine. As an Englishman he should have said it was time to take a fresh guard. It is high time he did so.

46 John Terry

On 5 February 2010, Fabio Capello, the Italian coach recruited by the Football Association to manage England for £6 million a year, went some way towards justifying his salary. He summoned John Terry to Wembley Stadium and sacked him as captain. The meeting lasted twelve minutes, and left the Chelsea player distraught. Terry reportedly wept as he pleaded with Capello to retain his badge. Having failed (the manager walked out of the room, leaving Terry to mop up his tears), he told a friendly newspaper that he felt 'gutted'.

To the rest of the country, even to those who had little interest in football, it was the only possible resolution of a shameful situation. Terry had betrayed his office, many times over, and had to go. Not just for having an affair with the ex-partner of a former teammate – inelegant though that was, with Terry paying for her abortion and the improper way he had sought to enrich himself while England captain. It went deeper than that, and people had come to the inescapable conclusion that, even by the desperately low standards that apply in football, he was an ill-mannered lout whose presence as the national team's figurehead was unacceptable.

The charge-sheet was long and unpleasant. On 12 September 2001, the day after the Twin Towers atrocity, Terry was one of a group of Chelsea players whose drunken behaviour in a Heathrow hotel reduced American tourists to tears. Four months later he was involved in an altercation with a bouncer at a members-only club in Knightsbridge. He was alleged to have struck the man with a beer bottle. Terry was acquitted when the case came to court, but controversy continued to dog him. There were tales of urinating in nightclubs, parking his car (a Bentley, naturally) in a disabled bay, and, as night follows day, of affairs with the kind of women who like to attach themselves to footballers.

When Capello appointed him captain in 2008, after a public audition, he was taking a punt. Terry had proved a forceful leader at Chelsea, where a banner displayed prominently on match days proclaimed him to be a club 'legend'. Isn't everybody these days? But he was also a graceless one, forever snarling at referees and linesmen if decisions went against his team. Moreover, when he missed a penalty kick against Manchester United that would have given Chelsea the Champions League in 2008, he wept. It was not exceptional behaviour, because many footballers enjoy nothing more than blubbing and abusing officials, but it did not mark him down as the heir to the office occupied by Billy Wright and Bobby Moore.

Unlike those men, who understood what an honour they had been granted, Terry never grasped what the captaincy of England meant. There were the usual platitudes, of course, but his behaviour gave the game away. Nor did the behaviour of his parents help. His mother was cautioned for shoplifting £800 worth of goods, and an undercover reporter exposed his father selling cocaine. When his admirers painted him as a Barking boy of solid East-End stock, this certainly wasn't what they had in mind.

Then came the avalanche of revelation that did for him. First, he was 'stung' by a newspaper, found taking £10,000 in £50 notes for showing punters round Chelsea's training ground in Surrey on the hush-hush. Terry's explanation that the money was earmarked for charity – minus a £2,000 cut for a ticket tout – was believed by few. If that were the case, why behave in such a clandestine way? Then a management company acting on his behalf offered his services to people who were looking for 'effective brand awareness'. Their client was, they boasted, a football 'icon', one of the most 'influencial' [sic] people in the world.

But at the end of 2009 he was named 'Dad of the Year' by Daddies Sauce. Not only was he a footballer supreme, he was also the model of domestic harmony, married to childhood sweetheart Toni. Surely everybody would want to be associated with such a man.

Oddly enough, away from the sort of nightclubs where they swig champagne at £1,000 a gargle, many people didn't want to do anything of the sort. The most damaging revelation, that the family man had conducted an affair with Vanessa Perroncel, a 'lingerie model', was so grimly predictable that the most appropriate response was laughter. The French-born model was the former girlfriend of Wayne Bridge, Terry's erstwhile teammate, and father of her child. At once she summoned Max Clifford, the public relations adviser, for a shoulder to cry on, and he announced that she would not be selling her story to the papers. Of course not – Terry, it was reported, had bought her silence.

This horrible tale had lurched by now into the world of self-parody, with everybody behaving badly, and, to be honest, there was some fun to be had. They all deserved one another. Yet one man was not laughing. As he sat in judgment, pondering the antics of a man in whom he had entrusted the game's greatest gift, Signor Capello found it all too easy to suppress a smile. For the sake of the team Terry had to go.

They saw things differently at Chelsea. They do at every club when one of their players has been wounded, for football is the most tribal of games. To them he remained 'JT', the great leader, the heart and soul of the club. To everybody else he was a foolish man who had been promoted above his station, and sullied the game he claimed to serve. It was a morality tale of sorts; a thoroughly grubby one.

47 Sir Harold Thompson

I n the autumn of 1977 English football was bumping along
the bottom. Liverpool may have won the European Cup in
Rome, to complete a journey that began thirteen years before
with the first of their championships under Bill Shankly, but
the national team had just lost its manager, Don Revie. Having
failed to qualify for the 1974 World Cup, they were soon to be
denied an appearance in the 1978 tournament. Scotland, it is
worth recording, qualified on both occasions.

It was Scotland's victory over England at Wembley in May
1977 that tipped Revie over the edge. He packed his bags for
the United Arab Emirates, leaving the Football Association to
think long and hard about his successor. They thought neither
long nor hard. Ron Greenwood, the former manager of West
Ham United, was invited to become a caretaker, and on the
basis of a victory over Italy, he was told to carry on. It was a
good day for the kindly Greenwood, a bad one for England.

The man who told him to carry on was Sir Harold Thompson,
a chemistry don at Oxford University, and the chairman of the
Football Association. Thompson had established Pegasus, the
club for Oxford and Cambridge graduates, in 1948 and worked

his way assiduously through the foothills of officialdom until he reached the sun-kissed summit. As FA chairman, his word was writ. A vain, touchy man, he referred to Sir Alf Ramsey by his surname, and bullied members of the FA staff.

Brian Clough, the clear favourite to succeed Revie, should have won the vote. But there was no vote. Thompson let it be known his mind was made up, and his colleagues fell meekly into line. 'If Ron Greenwood hadn't been around,' Peter Swales, one of the supine members of the international committee, said later, 'Clough would have won.'

It was a statement that beggared belief. Greenwood, well-meaning, highly regarded in coaching circles, and utterly weak, won the nomination ahead of Clough, who had proved himself to be a manager of outstanding quality. For what it is worth, he also enjoyed the overwhelming support of the public. English football has never known a more popular manager than Clough, yet this most practical of men came second to a theorist who could be guaranteed not to rock the boat.

Given his popular appeal, Clough had to be thrown a few fish, and so he was asked to look after England's youth team, which he did without much enthusiasm for a season. In his proper job he took Nottingham Forest, promoted the previous year, to their first championship, six years after he had taken Derby County to their first title. In 1979 he added the European Cup to his list of achievements, and Forest successfully defended their crown. Victory in Europe assuaged Clough's sense of grievance. In 1973 Derby overcame Benfica only to lose a fractious semi-final against Juventus, who, it was reported later in a *Sunday Times* investigation by Brian Glanville and Keith Botsford, had tried to influence the referee.

The intrepid men who served on the international committee were not to know that Clough would go on to enjoy such success, but that cannot excuse their timidity. Despite his acrimonious departure from the Baseball Ground, and the humiliation of his forty-four days at Leeds United, Clough's record of finding the best in players was no secret. They simply wanted a quiet life, and feared that Clough, an incendiary character, would light the occasional bonfire.

So they went instead with a man who could never take hard decisions. For his first match in charge, a friendly against Switzerland, Greenwood selected Ian Callaghan, Liverpool's veteran midfielder, instead of Trevor Brooking, whose career he had nursed at West Ham. As Glanville wrote in *The Sunday Times* after a grim goalless draw: 'Callaghan me no Callaghan. Brooking towers above him in sheer class.'

In his years at West Ham Greenwood had been a force for good. But he was an ineffective manager. 'Apply the principles!' he bellowed at his players during a game at Anfield. 'Did you hear that?' Bill Shankly asked his No. 2, Bob Paisley. 'They're going to apply the principles!' They applied them so thoroughly that they lost by four goals.

Even with Bobby Moore, Geoff Hurst and Martin Peters, three World Cup winners, Greenwood failed utterly to turn West Ham into champions, or anything like. So what on earth persuaded the FA that he could get the best out of international players? Greenwood couldn't even make up his mind about the goalkeepers. Peter Shilton, palpably superior to Ray Clemence, was obliged to share the jersey, match by match. It was ludicrous. After England left the 1982 World Cup at the quarter-final stage, Greenwood retired to Brighton.

Clough might have failed, just as Revie had failed, though that is unlikely. He had an unmatched talent for getting to the heart of the matter, and players loved working with him because he stretched them. He might have upset a few folk with ill-judged comments but he would not have picked a player like Glenn Hoddle, and then dropped him after he had scored a wonderful goal on his debut. Nor would he have tried to excuse his blunder by saying, as Greenwood did, that Hoddle was disappointed but 'disappointment is part of football'.

Sometimes a cliché rings true, and Clough was the finest manager England never had. Hats off to Sir Harold Thompson, who saw a saviour in Uncle Ron Greenwood, and got no more than he deserved. Peter Shaffer might well have written the final line of *Amadeus* just for him: 'Mediocrities everywhere [. . .] I absolve you all.'

48 Terry Venables

Terry Venables is the Chatterton of English football. Like Wordsworth's 'marvellous boy', the lad from Dagenham had established a gilded reputation before he reached adulthood. Capped by England at schoolboy, youth and amateur level he moved seamlessly through the under-23s to play for the national side at twenty-one. A year later he was a League Cup winner with Chelsea, and no sooner had he moved to Tottenham than he was an FA Cup winner.

Although his career never reached the snow-capped heights foretold by those heady early days, he remained a busy man on and, increasingly, off the field. He co-wrote four novels with Gordon Williams, which led to *Hazell*, a detective series on ITV. Then, when a coach's life beckoned, he struck oil at once. In 1979, at the age of thirty-six, Venables took Crystal Palace into the First Division, and the Glaziers were soon being talked up as 'the team of the Eighties'.

Talk is all it was. The Palace revolution lost its lustre when they went to Anfield, and found that the team of the Seventies had not yet finished their business. Liverpool scored three unanswered goals that afternoon, on the way to another

championship, and it didn't take Venables long to change tack. Back he went to QPR, where he had finished his playing career. He took them to a Cup Final in 1982, then won promotion to the First Division as he awaited the break that would make him.

It arrived in 1984, when the Ipswich Town board denied Bobby Robson permission to speak to Barcelona. Robson put in a word on the younger man's behalf, and soon Venables was off to Catalonia, where the Spanish championship was his within twelve months. The European Cup could also have been his a year later. It would have been Barca's first, a terrific feather to stick in his hat. But, after a poor match, and penalties, the cup went to Steaua Bucharest.

Back in England a year later he found a cosy billet at one of his former clubs. Tottenham won the FA Cup in 1991 on a day that is generally recalled for the two reckless tackles with which Paul Gascoigne effectively ended his career as a serious footballer. How Gascoigne left the dressing-room that afternoon in such an agitated state is unclear. It did not reflect well on the manager's ability to send his players on to the field in the right frame of mind.

On the whole, players spoke well of Venables, though their generosity did not help the master tactician to win any more trophies. While it is fair to say that success in management is about more than counting cups, a manager must be judged, to some degree, by his victories, and the facts reveal that in thirty years Venables won only two pots: the Spanish Championship with Barcelona, who tend to win quite a lot of them, and an FA Cup with Spurs, who are knock-out specialists.

It is a decent effort, but it hardly justifies the words lavished on his coaching ability by London scribes, many of whom have never found much fault with Venables. They still go on about his triumph at the European Championship in 1996 when, as England manager, he masterminded a 4–1 thrashing of Holland. It wasn't enough to keep him in the job, and soon he was off to Australia, who failed to qualify for the 1998 World Cup after squandering a two-goal lead to Iran in the qualifying play-off.

While he was the coach of Australia he moonlighted as chairman of Portsmouth. Venables had taken a controlling interest at Fratton Park for £1 in 1997, and left a year later £550,000 better off when he was bought out. In between engagements he was disqualified by the High Court from acting as a company director for seven years after he decided not to contest nineteen allegations brought against him by the Department of Trade and Industry. The court also imposed a fine of £500,000.

Hey ho. The yellow brick road took him immediately back to Palace, where he spent ten eventful months as manager. Recruited by Mark Goldberg, an ambitious owner, who called Venables 'the master of masters', he did very well out of the deal. We owe it to the investigative journalist, Tom Bower, for revealing how well. The club's offer included a five-year contract worth £3.5 million, a tax-free cash payment of £750,000, share options valued at £2 million, and £135,000 simply for speaking to Goldberg! A fat lot of good it did them. Palace were relegated, and Venables resigned.

The carousel still went round. Venables went to Middles-brough, to assist Bryan Robson for the better part of a season. Finally, in 2002, he was granted the job he had thirsted for in those fallow years. Leeds United, riding high in the Premier League and Europe, made him their manager. It was an unlikely liaison, which lasted all of eight months. The money available for David O'Leary wasn't there for Venables, though the customary pay-off, £2 million this time, made it a decent earner. As Bob Dylan sang, 'There's no success like failure, and failure's no success at all.'

For a time it was back to the television studio, to grin cheekily and mangle verbs. Not for ever, though. The Red Adair of football management was back with England in 2006, lending a hand to the beleaguered Steve McClaren. There were those who thought Venables should have been restored as England coach, but they were a small group by now, similar to the tribesmen of Papua New Guinea who worship the Duke of Edinburgh.

In the end the marvellous boy never became the grand old man of football. Wherever he went he was pursued by ghosts, whispering the words of Elizabeth Gloster QC, acting for the DTI in 1998. The conduct of Mr Venables, she told the High Court, 'has been such as to make him unfit to be concerned in any way with the management of a company'. Throughout his career football had taken a different view. What does that say about the game, and the people who run it?

The dying Chatterton was captured in a famous painting by Henry Wallis. It would be interesting to see if Venables keeps a portrait in his attic.

49 Ian Wright

In the autumn of his career Ian Wright played a few games for Burnley. It was difficult to imagine a more improbable club for somebody who had spent his life on both banks of the Thames, a point not lost on the lady reporter who travelled to witch country, in the lee of Pendle Hill, to lap up one of his appearances in a claret shirt.

Wright, she wrote, with the detachment of an anthropologist exploring some sub-Saharan heart of darkness, was bringing 'London cool' to a far-flung part of the world that obviously baffled her. The inference readers were invited to draw was that Lancastrians, who wore flat caps and talked funny, by 'eck, missus, mind me ferrets, should be glad to behold so wonderful a sight. Well, wouldn't anybody in the sticks admire Wright's 'awe-inspiring, almost alien presence'?

Perhaps she was thinking of the awe-inspiring way Wright had made obscene gestures to an Oldham fan, whose face he promptly covered in spittle. It was behaviour that brought the player a £1,500 fine from the Football Association, who also fined him £750 for spitting at a female steward at Queens Park Rangers. After making offensive gestures to fans at Coventry

the fine was £15,000. Indeed, those who kept a close watch on the player during matches were surprised he was not up before the beak more frequently, for he seemed to spend most of the time in a rage.

When he wasn't kneeing goalkeepers in the face, as Coventry's custodian Steve Ogrizovic claimed, or spitting at anybody within, well, spitting distance, Wright directed jibes at those odd folk who didn't see things his way. He called David Pleat, then the manager of Wednesday, 'a pervert', an odd choice of word from somebody who was so eager to pervert the spirit of the game, and – brave man – he even mocked a disabled linesman, Richard Saunders, during a game at Norwich.

The lady scribe could not possibly have forgotten Wright's coolness the afternoon he smashed up the referee's dressing-room at Upton Park after he had been sent off playing for West Ham against Leeds United. Or the cool way, as an Arsenal striker, he conducted his feud with Peter Schmeichel, the Manchester United goalie. Yes, he was one cool cat.

A stranger to shame, Wright carried this metropolitan chic into radio, when he was invited to spread a little happiness on (where else?) Five Live. Wrighty and 'Brighty' (Mark Bright) made such a well-matched pair, with a lacerating wit that recalled the Algonquin Round Table, that one can only regret their passing. The squealing in the studio made them sound like that other pair, Pinky and Perky, who, readers of a certain age will recall, sang 'We Belong Together'.

From Five Live it was a short step to the television studio, where Wright floundered like a trout on the riverbank. Initially the Beeb were delighted with their new signing. They even showed him leaping around the studio during England matches whenever 'we' scored a goal (an inexcusable lapse, given the supposed neutrality of summarisers) but his most star-struck admirers took a dim view when he refused to address Gary Lineker's question after an England defeat. 'I ain't sayin' nuffin', Links,' he said, turning his back on the presenter.

How on earth did a man with his record get a job on the BBC? Come now, have you never heard of 'diversity'? Here was a footballer who spoke in the tongue of urban youth. A 'character', no less. The fact that his antics alienated everybody over the age of eighteen was neither here nor there. Strutting, vapid 'Wrighty' was a catch, a steal, the real deal. How misplaced that confidence looks now.

Whatever one's standards, it would be surprising if they were satisfied by a man who used the phrase 'tits up' on a sports programme at lunchtime, or who told a former colleague: 'I made you the player you was', or who behaved as Wright did. Wright was not a fully-fledged England star like Gary Lineker or Alan Shearer, merely a very good club player. Let's speak to the urban youth – but abandoning one's standards and promoting a chump like Wright just patronises them.

In 2008 Wright flounced out of the BBC, claiming that he was regarded as a 'jester'. Who did he think he was? The Isaiah Berlin of the *Match of the Day* sofa, the George Steiner of White City? Anyway, off he toddled, with a parting shot to his former employers that people wanted their football experts to speak the language of the common man. Meaning, one supposes, they wanted to see the likes of Wright jumping on tables, pumping their fists and cheering on the lads.

It would be wrong to say he has been missed. The standards of football debate on television may be lamentable but even the dullest of dullards understood that Wright's punditry represented a step too far towards infantilism. He may be considered cool at TalkSport, his new home, and in certain parts of north London. In less progressive parts of the world they choose their adjectives more carefully.

50 Pini Zahavi

When Herbert von Karajan was simultaneously the music director of the Berlin Philharmonic and the Vienna State Opera, a regular visitor to Salzburg and Milan, and active in London and Paris, the joke went that every time he got into a taxi, and the driver asked where he wanted to go, he gave the same answer: 'It doesn't matter. They want me everywhere.'

The man who is wanted everywhere today is Pini Zahavi. This journalist-turned-agent is a conductor of a kind in the world he has made his own. Wherever he shows his face the fiddles are tuned, the flutes toot, and the trumpets ring like bells. He hardly needs to pick up the baton. Everybody knows how the piece goes.

Registered in Israel, where he began his working life as a humble footsoldier in the press corps, Zahavi spends much of his time in the dining rooms of Mayfair, and has a thorough knowledge of football's up-and-coming performers in Europe and South America. Players cross continents to have him by their side. Managers like to befriend him. If there's a deal to be done you can be sure that he knows both sides of it.

That agents are now the makers and breakers of clubs' fortunes is not in doubt. According to Premier League figures their fees for the 2007/8 season amounted to £66 million, which works out at £3.3 million a club. In this brilliant breaking of the bank everybody wins, sometimes twice over. It is not unusual for some agents to cut from both sides of the pack, so to speak. The only people who do not win are the supporters, who have become familiar with the summer beauty parade as players are hawked round to new owners every two or three years (while demanding their 'loyalty bonuses', of course).

It's a long time since managers could afford to order agents out of the door, safe in the knowledge that their word was writ. Some of them took money; that much was understood. Despite the prying eyes of official investigators a few still do. George Graham, sacked by Arsenal in 1995, was unfortunate in one respect: he was found out. Nobody seriously believes that the unsolicited 'gift' of £425,000 he received from the Norwegian agent, Rune Hauge, was the only one of its kind. Other managers have raked in millions from the sale of players.

In the mysterious world of transfers Zahavi is master of all he surveys. He is the king-maker who took Rio Ferdinand from Leeds to Old Trafford for £30m, acted as midwife in the bizarre operation that brought Carloz Tevez and Javier Mascherano to England, and, most significant of all, introduced Roman Abramovich to the game when he had pots of money and no clear idea of what to spend it on. Zahavi hasn't done badly for a man who began his working life reporting on players, not representing them.

To outsiders it is sometimes difficult to see exactly what agents do. Not the buying and selling, that's pretty straight-forward, but the stuff that follows. 'Rio is very happy,' Zahavi said as Ferdinand prepared to confirm an extension of his contract. 'He wants to stay, and they want him to stay.' In which case, why did the player need an agent? Wouldn't a nod and a shake of hands have been sufficient? Not really. 'They're babies,' Zahavi has said, speaking of the breed, not specifically the ones he looks after. And they will remain so, happy to be tucked up in bed and read a story if they're good.

It was Zahavi who attended Chelsea's liaison with Sven-Goran Eriksson, the England manager, in July 2003. That was the 'secret meeting', you may recall, the one that was in all the papers next day. He was also loitering in the restaurant when Chelsea met Ashley Cole two years later, though he made it plain that his presence was 'totally innocent'. He was speaking no more than the truth. In such a small world it would be surprising if an agent didn't turn up. These people all dine in the same hotels, drink in the same bars, and most are within staggering distance of the Piccadilly Line. How could anybody not believe him?

Zahavi makes no bones about it. His interests are 'football, football, football', in that order. Hence the courting of talented young players, like Ferdinand. Zahavi has twice done well out of him, moving the defender from West Ham to Leeds United before the transfer to Old Trafford. He supported the absent-minded Ferdinand through his eight-month ban for forgetting to take a drugs test in 2003, which left an indelible stain on the player's reputation. Ferdinand hasn't forgotten that debt. He even takes holidays in Israel. Zahavi has done well out of second-stringers, too. His share of Wayne Bridge's transfer from Chelsea to Manchester City in 2009 was £900,000. It's a fair old whack for a chap who wanted to get away.

The agent of stars has become a star agent. He hasn't broken any laws. He has observed the codes and customs of his trade, and brought in others from time to time to share a nibble from the rich man's table. By any standards he is superb at what he does. Even so, there is something faintly distasteful about the rise of the middle man, however good this one is. They should leave ripples. Zahavi leaves waves.

However fouled up it may be, football is still a game about footballers.